Summer of the Pigeon

volume one

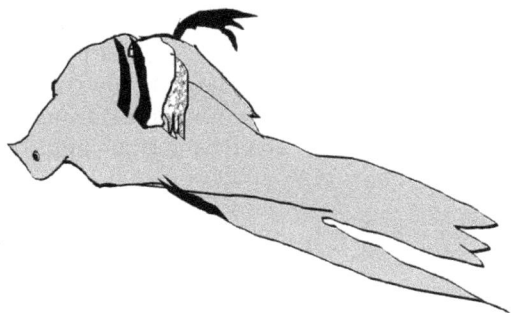

Kelly Frederick Mizer

It is not coincidental that you have stumbled across this book. I wrote it for you.   *-KFM*

· · ·

Printed by LULU.com
Published by loloINK www.loloink.com
October 2008

For Mom, Dad, and Christopher, a trifecta of love, and for Sean, my husband, whom I have loved since our first meeting, many years ago, in a cold painting studio in Manhattan.

Acknowledgements

There are many people who encouraged me throughout the process of writing this book. I'd like to thank my parents for being my sounding board after each entry. Dad, everything I learned about writing, I learned from you, and it was exciting to send you each new day, and wait for your response. I have saved all of your return emails and cherish your insight, humor, and honest feedback. Mom, you have been my cheerleader throughout, and your faith in me has given me such hope.

Thanks to my trusted friend T Ullrich, who took the time (along with my dad) to edit this work at the very last minute, and taught me the subtle art of the semicolon.

Thanks to Nick Hughes, principal at Wauwatosa East High School, who generously approved my job-share agreement. This work would not have happened without your support.

To the Mary Group, Jacque and Don Nelson, Rev. Martina Schmidt, Lori Sieren, and Dr. Rose Kumar, who reinforced my belief that there's no such thing as coincidence.

Thanks to my "birthday/book club" girls: Sue, Cathy, Anne, Kim, Pat for being the first to laugh at my stories and for giving me the confidence to get them down on paper.

A special thanks to Susie, who has been there for the stories that weren't so funny, who has always given me a safe place to land. I can't think of many things more delightful that drinking cold beer and eating mini donuts on a rooftop with you.

To my kids, of course, as these stories wouldn't exist without them, and to Sean, who is still holding onto the rope. I am honored to be your partner.

To Greta and her hunting instincts, and to the pigeon, who started it all and died with purpose.

"Once we believe in ourselves, we can risk curiosity, wonder, spontaneous delight, or any experience that reveals the human spirit."

-   e.e. cummings

June 6

So, today, our dog Greta caught a wounded pigeon. She wounded it further: took a leg off and some feathers. The poor bird continued to drag itself around our yard on one leg. I called my dad. He said, "Whack it with a shovel." I called Sean, my husband. He said, "Put it out in the middle of the street." I couldn't do either. Nope, couldn't do it. It was not a fly or a spider. It was breathing and scared and had sad eyes.

I called the Humane Society. That guy said to bring it in. "Bringing it in" would mean having to touch the thing. Anyone who has ever walked with me in New York or Washington D.C. or even Chicago knows how much I hate pigeons. HATE them, scary. I asked the humane society guy if I could pick the thing up with a shovel. He said a towel would be better, but I didn't even have to use one. I could just pick it up and put him in a box with holes. Fat chance.

So I find a shoebox and jab it full of the appropriate amount of holes for a dying bird (don't want to suffocate him, I reason, as that's a worse death than being bludgeoned to death with a shovel). I go to the spot where he is (under the swing set). I bring a shovel with me. I cannot bring myself touch him. He sees me and belly crawls over to the bushes. I try to scoop him up with the shovel. Can't be done. He is caught between some branches now. I keep trying and trying with the shovel. I say OUT LOUD, "Assistance *PLEASE*!"

He just stares at me. I tell him I am trying to help him, but he goes further into the bush. I'm going to have to pick him up. I get

William's (my youngest) catcher's mitt from the garage. I try to pick the thing up that way, but I just squish him and he flaps and bleeds. I bring out a piece of cotton fabric that I bought at the fabric store the day before. I try to pick him up with half fabric, half baseball mitt. It is raining now. Hard. It's humid and hot and I am tangled up in tree bushes.

After several minutes, I am able to pick him up. His one wing flaps away like crazy. I am freaked out. FREAKED OUT, but I tell him, "Okay, good, here we go. We've got it now, Pigeon!" I back up towards the slide. I trip on a giant rock. The box goes flying. I land on my head. The pigeon lands on me. He belly crawls away into the bush and I cannot find him. That's where he is now, decomposing, I suppose, in our garden. I took a shower and thought about salmonella.

When the kids and I came home from Montessori, William made some toast for the pigeon. He said that I simply could not leave it out to die. He asked to keep it as a pet. Feeling guilty now, we wedged it out of its hiding place (back by the telephone pole where William had placed the toast near the bird's tail feathers). We put it in the box with the holes on top. Together we drove Pigeon to the Humane Society where the guy told William that he'd take good care of him. Roughly translated, this means that the Humane Society has some really good drugs.

2

June 7

I have been having trouble handling summer heat ever since William was born during the hottest July of my life. Last night I felt like I was suffocating in my sleep. I was literally afraid of dying. I moved to the couch at 2 a.m. I thought about when I was three or four and we lived in Missouri and I loved summer. We would swim at the college pool. There were really high diving boards and those kicking boards shaped like fudgesicles. I remember that we had to take showers before entering the pool area, and I would always stand in the stall with my mom and complain about how hot she liked the shower water. Still, these were the best summers of my life, and if I could relive even one day, it would be to eat banana ice cream with my dad at that little stand we stopped by after swimming. I'd eat my cone in the back of my parents' blue Hornet. The seats were falling apart and sometimes my mom would sit, parked outside the house, sewing them up.

I am determined not to hate the weather this summer, to love things that I don't typically gravitate towards, like gardening and sewing. Last week Sean came home and I was sewing again. He said, "Jesus, what are you doing? Getting ready for the Great Depression?" So far, all the skirts I've made don't fit, and they are sloppy and crooked, so obviously homemade. Still, I would figure it out. I just don't want to use a pattern because they are written in such a stupid language. I don't know why they come with a key of symbols instead of a visual step-by-step guide, like what Ikea does for assembling cheap dressers.

But today I gave sewing a break and tried gardening. I usually avoid planting things, especially when it is hot. Just like my dad, and now my daughter, Elizabeth, if it is hot out and I am sweaty, my face turns bright red. I imagine that when I had William, I looked like a bloated and diseased Christmas elf. I decided to just deal with the heat and figure out the whole nature thing.

Elizabeth helped me garden. She seemed to get the rhythm of the whole thing much better than I did. She created a pattern: three red cone shaped flowers followed by three different types of purple ones. William punched her in the stomach because she didn't want him to pull out the tag that told us what kind of flowers we were planting. Every so often, I drank bad, sugarless iced tea (the bottle was sweaty and the tea had warmed) and checked my cell phone for missed alerts. When we were finished, I mowed the lawn and finished seconds before it started to thunderstorm and a tornado warning-siren sounded.

I don't know that this time of year will ever feel as satisfying as it did in the 1970's, but I did feel like saying, "Ta-da!" when I looked around at all of the flowers, even though Lizzie's "pattern" looked weirdly patriotic. Maybe, though, thirty years from now, Elizabeth will look back on the best summers of her life and fondly recall planting flowers with me. If that is the case, I have a renewed faith in the season.

June 8

Last week I stopped at a rummage sale because the sign in the yard read, "Vintage Rummage." I bought a thumb sized Virgin Mary. I bought this mainly for two reasons: I thought it was funny to think of Virgin Mary as vintage and because of the Beatles song *Let It Be*. I like the way the lyrics, "mother Mary comes to me," sound in my head. I hope that when the time comes, one of my kids is smart enough to know that this is the song I'd like played at my funeral. This song also makes me giggle because in seventh grade, I danced to it, awkwardly, with a boy named Ben, while our teacher danced in the background, Elaine Benes style.

Last night, I was humming that song on the porch, watching the rain. Luke, my oldest son (now the same age that I was during that first boy/girl dance) came out and sat next to me and offered me one earplug from his iPod. Together we listened to Rufus Wainright's *Hallelujah*. That song was played at my Grandma Jean's funeral, and whenever I hear it, I think about her, but now I am glad to also think about twelve-year-old Luke, the rain, and generosity.

June 9

It's still raining today. I came home yesterday and saw a wire loveseat on my porch. I thought Sean bought it, but it seemed like a weird purchase for him. Later, he was looking out the window and screamed, "Jesus Christ. What the fuck is on the porch?" He thought I bought it. We have a secret admirer, I guess. I spent the day at school accusing students via text (as my seniors have all graduated).

We found out tonight that our neighbors down the street left it for us as a surprise gift. I like these two neighbors very much. They live in an upper flat. One man is a florist and the other is retired. They own two wiener dogs, which is funny to me. They also ride their bikes everywhere, which is very NON-Wisconsin of them. I imagine them sitting on their upstairs patio, drinking Earl Grey tea and reading the New York Times. They have deep, guffawing belly laughs and seem to be very much in love.

At first I was very excited to see the loveseat because I believed that I had manifested it in the same way that the movie *The Secret* suggests is possible. I had just been thinking about clearing out the overgrown gazebo in the back and putting a bench there. Once I found out that it was from the Florist and Friend, I was even happier because I imagined I could invite them over for Gin Fizzes or Tom Collins once the gazebo project was finished. I would have to make absolutely sure though, that no Greta poop was in the yard. These are two men who should NOT have dog poop on their shoes.

Anyway, I heard Sean talking and the men guffawing and I went outside to join them to see if they were laughing about my pigeon escapades. They were. William came outside and finished a small painting for his teacher. We were out there for a long time until we realized that Luke was not home. Sean told me that he had seen Luke on Wells street and that Luke said he was going for a walk. Sean told him to make sure to ask me first, which he didn't. It was getting dark, and even if Luke had gone for a walk, he would have been home by now.

I called his friend Josh to see if he was there. Sean drove away in the blue pick up truck to find him. I stood on the sidewalk and waited and listened to the pulse of my heart and pushed out thoughts of what strangers do to twelve-year-old boys. Eventually, Luke wandered back, grasping a white paper bag of chocolates, purchased with his own money for his teachers, as an end-of-the-year thank you.

I feel uncomfortable knowing how easy it is for a life to change course; how I went from thinking about gin fizzes to thinking about child abduction in less time than in takes to say, "Thank God," out loud. It is frightening to doubt my intuition and I've decided not to think about the incident anymore. Instead, I will think about the peace that is generated by a young boy wanting to feel grown up, to purchase a gift with his own money, and to realize how it feels to give. Thinking about these things fills me up from my belly to my throat, like a prayer. Mother Mary, *comfort* me, whisper words of wisdom, let it be.

June 10

I am sunburned.

I remember my first bad sunburn was from a white water rafting trip that I took with my dad and his high school students when I was about eight or nine years old. The trip took forever and my poor dad had to do all of our paddling, as my efforts were pretty futile. He must have been so busy paddling that he didn't remember to put sunscreen on me; either that or sunscreen wasn't really "in" back then. By the time we came home, my back was raw and blistering and my mom was angry with my dad for bringing me home overdone. She put Noxema on me. I lay on my white alphabet sheets.

Many years later, when my family was just getting to know Sean, we all took another long and frustrating trip down the Wolf. The river was still that day, no rapids to move us along, and as I recall, Sean did all of our paddling. I couldn't figure out how to use those things in any productive way. It also didn't help that my contact lens fell out of my eye three quarters of the way into the ride. I believe that my version of hell includes a rubber raft.

Once, though, before the second Wolf run, Sean and I took a canoe trip with some friends in New Jersey. His friend Matt was supposed to bring the food, but he forgot the ice, so the mayonnaise on the sandwiches soured and we couldn't eat them. Matt also bought generic cola, which we drank warm. I knew that Sean would never in a million years buy generic cola and he also never would forget ice. He's the kind of guy that brings along rain ponchos to the Fourth of July fireworks, even if it's not supposed to rain. Though I already knew I loved Sean, it was on this canoe trip that I realized I could marry him one day. I knew he'd always pay for parking and he'd never use coupons. I know that some people list the traits they insist on in a partner (funny, honest, blah, blah, blah). I figure that stuff is a given (who is going to want a humorless liar?). I think it's important to be specific, so my list included "no coupons." When my friend Todd met Sean for the first time he said, "I like that Sean. He's the kind of guy who won't let go of the rope." I think that's the nicest compliment I've ever heard. I have loved him for nineteen years and he has never even loosened his grip.

June 11

Our lunch discussion at school today revolved around amusement park rides and we all fondly recalled The Edge, which was shut down soon after it opened because people kept dying on it. My friend, Kim, said she was there once and some guy broke his leg on The Edge and everyone was all pissed off because, despite the fact that the scene was full of ambulances and camera crews, it was taking too long to get the ride up and running again. I reminded Kim of how that clip of Fabio getting hit in the face with a goose while he was on a rollercoaster gets shown over and over again on TV and we all laughed as Kim mimicked Fabio's stunned and bloody face. Another teacher, Barb, said that she's surprised that the impact of the goose didn't kill Fabio and then she said, "Geese bring down entire airplanes, you know!" I had never heard of that and I don't think I believe her.

My colleague, Jim, said that he often wonders why birds don't hit him in the face when he rides his bike, as he is always getting hit in the face by bugs and branches and other things. I think maybe Jim should stop riding his bike.

I wonder if Fabio ever had a fear of birds before he took that memorable rollercoaster ride. Maybe his psyche forced the event to happen. I am positive that the reason I broke my foot a few years back is because even thinking about twisting an ankle has freaked me out since 1993. Maybe Jim will get hit the face with a beak next time he rides his bike to work and maybe Barb's plane will be destroyed by a lone goose. As I sipped my vanilla Italian soda, I wondered what irrational fears Kim has, as I can't recall her ever mentioning any, except for the fact that she can't sleep with pants on. I don't know if that is a fear though or just a comfort thing.

When I don't sleep with pants on, I fear a fire will drive us out onto the street and I will be wearing one of those silly t-shirts that Sean's mom always gives me. The latest one is green and has a beaver on it and reads "Dam Tired." When I saw the beaver, I was relieved to see the text referred to real animal beavers and not their slang counterparts.

June 12

Everything in this house is broken. There isn't a room to be found without something that needs major work. Once I videotaped William giving me a tour of broken windows. In each room, I asked him how the window got broken. Sometimes the answer was "a ball," but my favorite answer was when he said that he was pretending to be a birdie.

I believe the weight of the daunting task of fixing the broken parts inside is what has driven me to garden outside (though the garage windows are broken too, as is the umbrella over the rusted patio furniture). It's still raining though, so I cannot garden. Most of the state is flooded. The flowers that Elizabeth and I planted are flat against the ground now. So today I was stuck inside and decided to gut the attic and the kids room and shoot for a Saturday rummage sale. I found several boxes labeled "Favorite Lizzie Clothes." I don't know what I was thinking, but I must have saved everything she ever wore, including baby tights. Now it is all sitting in our living room, priced to sell. Sean told me that he couldn't help on Saturday though, so maybe I'll just do a Goodwill run instead.

As I cleaned out the attic, I had visions of turning it into a little playroom for the kids, but seeing that we have lived without a kitchen for fifteen months now, I suppose I shouldn't consider any more projects. I don't know why Sean hasn't worked on the kitchen because it would literally take him three days to do. He frequently says he will never put anything nice in our house because none of us know how to clean. It's the typical "shoemakers kids have no shoes," story, but seriously, fifteen months? That's longer than it takes to grow twins and get them sleeping through the night.

There are some things that Sean and I will never ever agree on: baby names, the color walls should be, a dream vacation spot, or how to drive. I sometimes think that people who are close to me think that I am the one who has made some pretty big compromises, the kitchen being a prime example. I'd like to agree with that, but I can't. Sean moved a thousand miles to be with me. He hasn't celebrated a holiday with his parents in his hometown since Luke was born. He gave up his preferred side of the bed for me. When I was on bed-rest for thee months with Elizabeth, he pushed my bed to the middle of the room and repainted it because the green color was making me crazy. Sometimes he does mean things and sometimes the mean things he says are funny (like yesterday, when he said, "Jesus. Nice necklace. What is that? A sundial?")

Still, it's okay with me for crabbiness to set in. I have gotten used to his comments on my overall choice of clothing. My friend Sue says at least he notices what I am wearing. Once I wore a big crocheted sweater and he said, "Well, if that doesn't say art teacher all over it, I don't know what does." Whenever I wear my teal pants, he calls me Jaclyn Smith, and no matter how many times he has seen me wear the same shoes, he says: "I see you got another pair of shoes." So, yeah, he notices. To be fair, he makes the same kind of comments about his own life and about pretty much everyone else's too. When we lived in Colorado, the people in the townhouse next to us were always up early working on their house and Sean would roll over in bed and say, "Damn do-it-yourselfers." When the man told Sean at the gas station, "I'm going to get the Mercedes detailed today," Sean got back in our car and said, "Well, pin a rose on you." What I'm getting at is that I don't take these comments personally.

So everything is broken, but I don't take the blame for it and I suppose I don't really blame Sean either. I think it's a mixture of things that have built up. In the time we've lived here, we've had three children (two of them back to back), Sean has started his own business, and we've each had a surgery. Even Lizzie had a surgery. We've gotten Luke through vision therapy and William through psychotherapy. We've changed schools, made friendships, learned a thing or two; cleaning and fixing just hasn't been a priority. I still look at photographs of nice homes and clean rooms, but I also appreciate that our friend Mike calls *Real Simple* magazine, *Real Simple if You're Rich and Bored*. However, Mike does have a flawless house himself.

The kids are older now. I don't have to bathe anyone. No one wakes me up in the middle of the night. It's time to put the energy into our surroundings. I started with the attic. It's an appropriate place to begin.

June 13

A few summers ago when William was only four, I banned Dairy Queen. I was in the drive thru line and asked for a scoop vanilla ice cream with a few M&M's on it. They would not put M&M's on it. They said M&M's were only for Blizzard drinks. I argued that they had the candy right there, couldn't they just put two small candy coated chocolates on the very top to please my small son? The rest of the conversation went very much like the Jack Nicholson's request for toast in *The Five Easy Pieces*. After much debate, I lost, but I told them to cancel my entire order and that I would never, **ever** return. My children were stunned and they haven't forgotten that 2005 was the year I banned Dairy Queen forever. I hadn't counted on them remembering, which kind of sucks, because every once in awhile I want a chocolate dipped cone. My kids never questioned the decision; it seemed to make so much sense to them that this kind of injustice would receive a harsh punishment.

Tonight we drove to McDonald's very late at night as we missed dinner (with all the rummage sale preparation). I had ordered a filet-o-fish for Elizabeth. Our order was not even close to ready when we pulled up to the second window and so they asked us to pull ahead because the fish wasn't done. We waited an unusually long time, just William and I in the car. I finally said under my breath, "What are they doing? Killing the fish themselves?" William asked, "They kill fish in there?" I explained no, not really, I was just getting impatient. Then William, under his own breath said, "Good, because if they killed fish, we'd have to ban them too."

15

June 14

The rummage sale was pretty successful, the rain held out, and I am even more sunburned. We set up at about six thirty a.m. at which time our neighbor across the street made fun of us by asking if we were collecting appliances.

It is always interesting to see who comes to rummage sales, who stops their cars, who says hello, who smiles. My favorite guy was toothless, weathered, sparkly character who was very excited to see that we had so many old things. He bought a ton of junk. He said, "I'll take the boat anchor too," and I don't know if he was being serious or sarcastic, as the big metal thing he bought was certainly not a boat anchor. He ended up buying the one thing that was hard for me to see go: a broken fireplace screen that I originally purchased at Goodwill for nine dollars. This surprised me, to feel a pang of "goodbye" to a lousy old thing (especially when I had no qualms about selling all of the kids baby clothes and Christmas firsts).

The fireplace grate, however, is related directly to one of my favorite Sean moments. At the end of last summer, a chipmunk found his way into our kitchen wall. We could hear him squeaking away. He eventually made his way through the big opening in the wall (where the sink used to be) and Sean spent the night trying to catch him. Sean made the rest of us stand outside on the deck so that he could really focus on chipmunk sounds. From outside, we could hear tables being turned over, some broken glass. We waited out there forever. Sean tried desperately to catch him so that he could release him back outside. By the time the rest of my family tired of waiting it out on the hot deck, Sean was drenched with sweat and armed with the aforementioned disassembled fireplace screen and a broom handle. He looked like a crazed pirate. I watched with apprehension and disbelief as Sean lay on the ground with a flashlight, peering under our radiator, waiting for his moment. A couple of times, he did get the chipmunk onto the screen with a spatula and then he would yell, "Get the bucket! Get the bucket!" The chipmunk always wiggled away just in time.

The last time, he wasn't as lucky. Instead of using the broom to guide him onto the screen, he slammed the broom on the ground in front of the chipmunk, as to stop him in his tracks. Sean was a split second too late though, and the broom landed on our little chipmunk, killing him. Sean was a force field of grief, despair, and anger. "I fucking killed it! I killed the fucking thing. Fuck. Oh, fuck," over and over again.

Since then, the dented fireplace screen has sat in our garage, until today. My favorite customer gave me four quarters for it and put it into the back of his truck, while his dog waited in the front seat. As he drove away, I longed to tell him the true history of why is was dented and why it was worth more than a dollar, but I just let him drive off. I hope he uses it. I hope he makes something with its parts. Something beautiful.

June 15

Today was Father's Day. I heard William wake up early and shake Lizzie. They went downstairs and attempted to make coffee. I woke up to help them. Without a kitchen, we couldn't really cook breakfast for Sean, but William suggested we microwave a hotdog. We went for a toasted English muffin instead, even though Will had a hard time understanding why adults might not be in the mood for hotdogs at 7:00 in the morning.

Elizabeth drew a large picture of an Alaskan Husky for Sean, which he mistook for a cat. She gently taped the drawing onto the fireplace and signed it, "Much Love, Elizabeth." I thought that was interesting because that is always how I sign cards and I guess she has paid attention.

After the morning ended, I drove my car full of rummage sale leftovers to Goodwill. I smile every time I think of Goodwill because the first time William heard me use that word was when I was donating his outgrown clothes that he did not want to part with. He pleaded with me, "but Mom, I *am* a good Will," thinking that I was giving them away because he was a bad Will. On my way there today, he told me that he couldn't stand the thought of me giving away Lizzie's baby shoes and to "please, please save them." I had already buried these shoes deep into a lawn sized garbage bag and didn't feel liking digging for the "needle in the haystack." Still, when I got to Goodwill, I felt sad about the shoes and even though there was a long line of people behind me waiting to drop off their junk, I stopped to dig through the bag and pull out two impossibly tiny black patent leather shoes. When I arrived back home I was so excited to show them

18

to Will. I said, "I realized these are important to you, so we will save them for when you have a baby many years from now." He took one glance at the shoes and said, "Those are two different shoes." He was right. Though they both were patent leather, one had a heart on the bottom of the sole and they had different kinds of clasps. Two left feet. Sometimes I am not such a good mom.

We all had an early dinner at my parents. Afterwards, William learned to ride his bike without training wheels. He was very proud (especially because he figured it out so quickly) and anyone watching him could tell that he felt free. Being the oldest myself, I never understood how difficult it must be to be the baby of the family and having to bear witness to everyone else's victories first. That would kill me personally, having to wait. For years now, I have called William "Caboose." Today, though, he was leading the pack and I knew that every cell in his body was filled with pure, sweet joy. I watched him race down the vacant country road, long blond hair blowing in the summer wind, until he was nearly out of sight, ending the most memorable of Father's Days. He is, indeed, a very good Will.

June 16

My eyes have been bothering me so much today. They are burning and watering like mad. This has never happened to me and it feels like I got soap in my eyes, except I didn't. I assumed it was "allergies," even though I don't really have allergies. Later, I walked to the bathroom to rinse out my contact lenses. It was then that I realized the bottle I have been using is not contact solution; it is nasal spray. Here's hoping I'm not blind by tomorrow.

It has been a bad health day all around. My mom ended up in the emergency room for many hours with what ended up being some infection from a bug bite or another unknown source. I'm betting it was a deer tic because yesterday when I was at her house, I stepped in deer poop.

My mom doesn't get sick very much and she rarely does stupid things, like washing contacts in poison (although she did wear two different shoes to work once, which I find comforting because I have done that as well). My mom did get sick last month, however; she had appendicitis. So today was a bit scary because it was the second time she's been in a hospital not only in a short time span, but in my entire memory. I panicked for a brief second (especially because the newscaster Tim Russert, also fifty-eight, died this week) thinking about what I would do if my mom died. After all the terrible stuff I thought about (like how there wouldn't be any sour cream twists on Christmas morning), I cried, which didn't help my eyes any at all, so instead I thought that if my mom died, I would plant poppies because she loves poppies.

Later I distracted myself, waiting for my dad to call with news, by starting work on the gazebo project. I dug out a lot of weeds, but I didn't know what tools to use to cut back all of the overgrown trees. I knew that Sean used a chainsaw once, but I decided that because I am the kind of person who poisons her eyes and can't match shoes one hundred percent of the time, that I might not be the chainsaw type. I did look at the chainsaw for a while and noticed that it seemed to start much like the lawn mower does, but I stopped short of actually using it. I Googled "pruning trees," and learned what a lopper was, but was disappointed to know that we don't own a lopper. Sean said I just need a sharp garden sheers and I told him that I tried to use our garden sheers, but they are so rusty they couldn't cut dog poop. He said that I didn't try using garden sheers, but that what I used was a grass trimmer. I have a lot to learn about garden tools.

When my dad called to say that my mom would be okay, I took a break from the yard work and lay down with a drippy warm washcloth over my eyes and listened to Luke rehearse the lyrics to *Joseph and the Amazing Technicolor Dreamcoat*, the play he auditioned for today. I felt heavy and sad, Lizzie's violin notes from out on the porch just a bit fainter than Luke's singing. William brought me a vanilla ice cream bar dipped in chocolate (our version of Dairy Queen) and together we sat and I sighed. He curled up into me, knowing, I believe, how much it matters to have   a   mother.

21

June 17

I did a lot of driving today. I had a reiki appointment and then had to go to the doctor to hear the results of my third MRI, which was basically inconclusive, and now I have to go for an ultrasound. Reiki was really good though. I felt my throat open up and I thought about stuff I'd long forgotten.

For dinner, Sean and I ate outside at this little place by our house. It wasn't very good and the service was really slow. For some reason the last several times that we have eaten out, it has taken forever. Ultimately, Sean ends up mumbling something like, "Could have flown to Jersey by now." Plus, we ordered glasses of wine, but the glasses only got filled up a quarter of an inch. I hate that. "I ORDERED A GLASS OF WINE, NOT A DIXIE CUP OF WINE," I want to shout, but instead I just say, "Thank you."

At one point, a lady carrying a large, clear garbage bag full of fat goldfish passed us. I wondered where she got them from and where she was walking to, but got distracted by the conversation that was taking place next to us, which was about pumping breast milk. The husband wanted to know how much five ounces really was. After seeing the fish and thinking about breast milk, I wasn't very hungry, especially for pumpkin ravioli in sage butter, which seems like a very odd thing to have on a menu in summertime.

Come to think of it, the entire menu was very fall-like. Sean had pork topped with mulled apples, served over spinach. That is a weird thing to eat outside and it made me feel depressed and anxious. I was more in the mood for sweaty glasses of iced tea and a perfect fruit and cheese plate.

The food didn't sit well with me and I regret having any wine at all, as I was instructed to drink lots of water after reiki. Once I had wine after an intense acupuncture session that a friend's aunt performed on me in the middle of Central Park. She, too, told me to drink lots of water. She also told me that my shoes were irresponsible and that I had "mother's syndrome," which lead me to ignore her advice. When I woke up in the morning, my tongue was black and made me think of squid's ink and my face was swollen and bruised. I hope that doesn't happen again.

Days like this (driving and waiting, driving and waiting) make me feel like I haven't accomplished anything much at all. Though I did finally do a bunch of laundry, as Sean keeps complaining about the serious lack of underwear in his drawer. I washed all of his underwear. He asked me how many pair that was and so I counted them. Ten. He has ten pairs of underwear neatly folded in his top drawer.

After tomorrow there will be only nine.

June 18

Elizabeth broke her wrist tonight. No swimming. NO SWIMMING! No swimming lessons, no swimming at Wirth park, no swimming at Pewaukee Lake, no swimming at her friend's house. That's the one that really got her. Dailey's birthday party-swim-extravaganza is on Saturday and Elizabeth didn't think of that until the doctor started to put her cast on and that's when she started to sob. They offered her a blue sling or a pink sling and she chose blue. The doctor said, "Oh, really. Wow. All little girls like pink."

"I don't," she said.

Two nights ago she woke up screaming because there were ghosts in the room. She said that one of them was moving her table. I told her to go back to sleep, that she was dreaming, just dreaming. She insisted that her eyes were open and that she was not dreaming, so I stayed with her because truth be told, I could sense a presence in the room as well and I remember being her age and seeing things like that and no one believing me. When I was three and living in Missouri I saw all of the characters on my Bambi pillow come to life. I made my mom throw out the pillowcase in the middle of the night. Over a decade later, I found it folded in a linen closet in Wisconsin and felt so betrayed. So I stayed.

When I wrapped my arms around her, she said that my skin smelled like root beer floats. She cuddled into me, her waist-length brown hair covering my neck. Her arms are long and lanky, with no trace of toddler flesh left, and she smelled like coconuts and plums.

June 19th

William and I have been fortunate enough to have lots of alone time each morning, as Luke and Elizabeth are at play practice each day from eight to noon. We always pick a spot for coffee and then discuss how we should spend the next few hours. Usually, William chooses to go to Alterra for breakfast because they have a flower shop next store that has gumball machines. The gum has Nerds candy inside of it.

The last two mornings we have gone to Steins to get stuff for Project Gazebo. He likes going to the garden store, mostly because they sell Webkinz and suckers, but he has also been a really big help and is very patient, looking at flowers. Today I told him that I really appreciated all of his help and I would let him pick out whichever flowers he wanted. He picked all yellow ones: daisies, marigolds, and daylilies. He was so excited about the daisies. I even tried to talk him out of them, as I am not such a fan of yellow, but he said that they were his favorites. He gently picked up each pot and set it on top of the patio bricks that we had stacked on our cart. He dragged the heavy cart, by himself, to the front of the checkout line. It took a really long time because the bricks weighed about twice as much as William, but he was so proud of his work that he insisted on pulling everything.

When we got home, I planted all of his yellow flowers. Thirty seconds later, Greta ate them. William cried. He chased the dog around the yard, screaming until we it was time to pick the other kids up from practice.

When Lizzie got in the car, she burst into heavy sobs because her cast was so hot and itchy and she had to "just sit and watch while everyone else did things with their hands!" She told me that she didn't cry all morning, that she waited for me to cry.

The tears continued periodically throughout the day. Lizzie's always revolved around her "stupid, stupid cast," and William's were triggered by all sorts of things: Luke "almost killed him," we were out of strawberry cream cheese, his bagel had two bottoms instead of a top and a bottom, no one wanted to play tag anymore, and he missed the ice cream truck. I think that today my children cried more in eight hours than I have in the last decade. Luke didn't help matters either, as every ten minutes he asked me when I was going to make his costume for the play.

It is starting to get dark out now. Bedtime. Finally. When Lizzie was little, she would sing, "He's got the whole world in his Hands," before she slept. She would sing things like, "He's got bunnies and kittens in his hands, He's got bunnies and kittens in His hands . . ." until William would interrupt her and sing his own lyrics: "He's got trains and seaweed in his hands, trains and seaweed." He's got the whole world in His hands: crying children, itchy casts, dead marigolds, and exhausted me.

June 20

Luke is nervous about the play. I would be too, especially if I had to wear a pharaoh suit and imitate Elvis Presley. I could barely stomach the idea of dancing at my own wedding; I've never even danced alone in my room. I don't sing in the shower and I stop singing along with the radio if I am at a traffic light. I can't imagine singing and wiggling my hula-hoop hips on stage in front of an audience. I couldn't even do that drunk.

Luke has been humming the lyrics, reading the lyrics, downloading different versions of the song on Youtube. He takes long showers and molds his hair into Elvis pompadours. He says, "Thank you, thank you very much," to no one in particular. I made his costume today. Twice. The first time he didn't like it because it was a dress. Pharaoh or no pharaoh, twelve-year- old boys and "dresses" are out, even when one insists it's a robe, not a dress. Then I tried deconstructing some old t-shirts. I used Lizzie's sewing machine to make fancy Egyptian shapes all over the place. I used all of my thread. Luke didn't like the way it felt ("too big"). I gave up. I poured glitter all over a white t-shirt. He was happy with that.

William and I shopped at rummage sales all morning. At one place we found a daisy costume. The headband had white petals all around it and Will suggested that Luke could wear it around his neck as part of his costume. It was a great idea and we were both excited about it. Luke hated the idea, even after I took all the petals off and sewed them into hieroglyphics (costume number two).

I remember being twelve. I know that Luke is starting to feel things deeply; he is suddenly aware of his identity. Doubt is starting to replace self-assuredness, not always, but enough. It's a pause, a hesitation that exists in most adults. So I am treasuring this play because I don't know how long his willingness to take this leap of faith will last.

When I was at reiki last time, I noticed a photograph on the wall. It was of Martina (my energy healer) standing in front of red Sedona rocks. Her arms were outstretched and she was smiling towards the sky. It dawned on me that it was the exact same pose I always took in front of any camera when I was young. The last photo I have of myself like that, arms wide open, celebrating me, was taken on my thirteenth birthday, a year older than Luke. My dad gave me flowers that day because he wanted to be the first man to ever give me any. I understand, only now, that it was more than that.

June 21

Today marks summer solstice; happy anniversary to us. Sean gave me a "Lawn Buddy" this morning: a plastic wagon full of brand new shiny garden tools. In a million years, I never expected to get excited about such a thing, but I have turned a new leaf. Traditionally, I am aware, wedding anniversaries are celebrated with things like tin, paper, silver, and gold. I think that we should make it official. Year Eleven: Garden Tools.

It was an unusual day because even though we filled it up (playing with puppies at a kennel, eating fancy dinner with William, going to a fun bonfire) I felt kind of removed from everything. I have had a slight headache most of the day and it almost felt like the real me is out of my body, hovering above the physical me, waiting.

We started the day by going out to Alterra for coffee and potato burritos. On the way there we passed a church that was advertising vacation bible school. Elizabeth asked us what a bible was. I learned that it is hard to explain what a bible is.

It got me thinking about how when Elizabeth was younger she always wanted to know how we got here ("not how babies are made, Mom, but how we ALL got here in the first place"). I would share with her different theories, but admitted that no one really knew for certain. She asked me what I thought God looked like and I told her that I didn't think God looked like anything in particular. She said that she believed God just was "two big hands up in the sky moving us around like chess pieces."

If that is true, and in fact He really does have the whole world in His hands, today felt like I had been lifted up without much commitment, a lone, headachy pawn in midair, waiting to drop into place, while the distracted hands contemplated where and whether or not to drop me.

June 22

We are all covered with mosquito bites from the bonfire. Elizabeth, in particular, has a ton. When I brushed her hair tonight, she made me brush her back too, to relieve some of the itching. Afterwards, she brushed my hair for a long time. When my cousin Laura and I were very little we would stay at Lolo's house, wear her nightgowns, and take turns brushing each other's long hair. Many of the rituals I have putting my own kids to bed comes from those nights with Laura: drawing imaginary letters on their backs, lightly dusting their eyelids with my fingertips, tickling their forearms. I think that one of the most intimate relationships I've ever known was on those few nights that my aunt Janice let Laura stay at Grandma Lois's too.

I have been trying to reconnect to the person I have always been. I have a picture of myself on my bedroom mirror. I am standing in front of my first stretched canvas, wearing a Holly Hobby sweatshirt, blond ponytail low at my neck, and my eyes are connecting to the camera in a way that, still today, shows my most honest self. I was probably five in that photo. I keep it on my mirror as a way to remind myself that I am still that same person.

There are many little things that I think about when trying to connect: my first days-of-the-week underwear, scribbling black crayons over a rainbow page to make my own scratch art, the summer road trips we took, drinking cream soda in the back of Lolo's hot olive green Oldsmobile, sleeping in her bed (staring at Jesus), playing Blockhead, wonton parties. These are little things. There are bigger ones, like sitting in our 56th street bathroom with my dad learning the difference between translucent, transparent, and opaque, my mom's macramé that hung on their bedroom wall, my mom asking me if I would like a brother, Silver Dollar City, Snake River, riding in the orange child seat on my dad's ten speed.

I have been realizing lately, though, that all these thoughts are from before the age of eight or nine and I cannot remember those same feelings of self from much later than that. I think it was around then that I started living from the outside in, rather than the other way around. I'm not sure what changed because even the big events in my life (my wedding day, childbirth) don't give me that same sense of knowing who I am in the way that banana ice cream does.

There was a moment, just after Elizabeth was born. Just the two of us were in the room and we fell asleep, her seven-pound body on my chest and I felt "it." I felt plugged in and whole. She was the only baby of mine that got to stay in the room with me, the boys being so premature that they were whisked away immediately. I lay with Elizabeth that way for hours until one of the nurses woke me up and scolded me for not feeding the baby.

Eight years later, as Elizabeth brushed my hair, I thought about how I'd like to invite myself back in; to trust myself, to be vulnerable enough, to open. I'm not sure where or how to begin, but I think I will start by buying the same kind of nightgown that Lolo wears: sleeveless polyester pseudo-silk and knee length.

June 23

Today I have been cursing the family that lived in this house before we did because when they remodeled the kitchen (badly), they got rid of the clothes chute. Who in their right mind would bury a clothes chute? I believe it is the best invention ever made and I'd sooner live without air conditioning (which I do) than without one. I hate laundry. I hate matching socks. I hate paying for laundry detergent only to run out of it so quickly. I think I hate it because there is never a "ta-da" moment (which is also why I don't like taking walks without a destination). It's an endless cycle. The only fun part is pulling the lint from the dryer screen. That, I find immensely satisfying.

In general, I find cleaning a bore. Once I had to take a class to renew my teaching license. It was called "Stress Management." It was a ridiculous waste of time because basically the guy just showed PBS movies for eight hours a day and made us take walks in search of a tree to hug (not kidding). On the first day, we all had to sit in a circle and talk about ways that we each relieve stress (one can see how this $800 three credit course would make me a much better teacher). Anyway, at least nine of the women there said that cleaning helped them reduce stress. I still can't believe that. I wanted to say that one way I would be glad to reduce stress would be to take the money I was using to get recertified and invest it into a cleaning service,

but I figured I had to pass the class, so I just mumbled something like "shopping" instead.

I remember that in high school I babysat for some friends of my dad's. The wife had a list taped above her sink that listed the days of the week, each day had chores listed with it. Things like "washing the curtains" and "changing bed skirts" were listed bi-weekly. I decided right then and there that I would not ever lead a life that revolved around a chore list. If I had to wake up, walk to the kitchen sink, run water for coffee and then read, "Wednesday: wash toilets," I'm pretty sure I'd put a gun to my head.

Growing up, I had two terrifically opposite grandmothers. Grandma Jean's house was a mess, always. Lolo's was perfect. She even rotated the sofa cushions every few days so that they would stay firm and even. I liked being in both houses. The dichotomy was powerful to me, even then. The best part of both of their houses was their bathrooms. Lolo had a clothes chute in hers. The room smelled like baby powder. All the matching towels were folded neatly in the linen closet and there were mirrors and framed drawings of bunnies everywhere. Toothbrushes hung inside the wooden vanity, and it was always fascinating to play with all of the little bottles of perfumes and makeup in the drawers. When I was pregnant with Elizabeth, I always had dreams of giving birth in Lolo's bathroom. My grandma Jean's bathroom didn't even have a door. Maxi pads and electric water picks, Dixie cups and magazines were everywhere. It smelled like vitamins.

It surprises me that my house now is more like my Grandma Jean's version. Today, I understand that at least 90% of her mess stemmed from the fact that she did not have a clothes chute either. I find some comfort in knowing that all of her children grew up to have fabulously neat houses. At least one day, I will have great places to visit.

June 24

My heels are cracking. It is painful.

Aside from newborn babies, Sean has the smoothest feet I have ever seen, not one flaw. I don't know when my feet started to crack at the heel, maybe fifteen years ago or so. Each time I take a step, it feels like someone is shoving a piece of glass in there.

One time when Sean's mom was visiting, she saw my feet and gasped in horror. She immediately went out and purchased creams and pumice stones. She said that I needed to take better care of myself. I suppose that is true, but it also explains why Sean has such smooth feet. That, or the fact that he wears heavy socks with sneakers year round. He even sleeps with socks on. I believe there are two types of people in this world, the socks-to-bed type, and the rest of us who think that's crazy.

I remember having a student a number of years ago that complained of having to go to her friend's house because she had hardwood floors. I couldn't imagine someone not loving hardwood floors, but Katharine said they always felt dirty under her feet and that she'd rather be at her house where the carpet was plush and inviting, and vacuum scars were proof that the floors were clean. Katharine wore socks to bed too. I know because I asked.

Lolo does not wear socks to bed. I remember her coming home from work and propping up her huge, distorted feet onto a little white vinyl ottoman. Her dog, Buffy, would lick and lick those feet. And my Grandma would laugh because it tickled her. She would occasionally shoo Buffy away, but most of the time, she'd let her come back, and Lolo would sit, drinking a Pabst

Blue Ribbon beer from a glass, Readers Digests stacked neatly next to the lamp at her side, Buffy licking away during the entire newscast.

Greta licks my feet now. Sean thinks that it is disgusting, but for me, it's just a lovely reminder that even though my feet are damaged goods, I am Lois's granddaughter.

June 25

The other day, right before Lizzie broke her wrist, I overheard a conversation that she was having with Willie. She was asking him what his favorite beer was, to which he replied, "I like wine." She told him that she likes Guinness best, but after a few minutes admitted that she had never really tried Guinness, but her "daddy drinks it" and she "smells it on his breath and it smells delicious."

That made me think about the time I was sitting at Conijitos bar with my uncle Patrick (who is only a few years older than me) and he was talking about growing up without his dad. I asked him if he remembered anything at all about him before his death and he said, "I remember the way his whiskers felt on my cheek and the way his face smelled."

Smell is funny that way. Awhile back, I went with our former principal to visit other local high schools to check out their Tech. Ed. Departments. When we walked into the woodshop, I took a deep breath and said, "Oh, I love that smell. It smells like my husband." The principal laughed and laughed because he didn't think husbands should smell like sawdust and motor oil. He didn't think it was a good smell. I don't know if he realized that he, himself, smelled like cigarettes, cologne, and drycleaner's plastic. Not that there's anything wrong with that.

I am in love with the way people I am close to smell. Susie, like rosewater. My mom, like musk and oil paint. Kim, Aveda. Cathy, Lemongrass. I grew up loving that my aunt Shirley smelled like Tide. It is the only laundry soap I will buy now and I am quite sure that I am drawn to sandalwood, cedar, and jojoba because my Aunt Lori always smelled like she had bathed in essential oils for hours, like an Egyptian queen. But Lizzie is right on, the lingering smell of Guinness on Sean's lips, mixed with sawdust and motor oil is just about the best thing around.

Thinking about Pat losing his dad at four years old makes my whole heart sting and radiate pain right up to my throat. Yet I am glad to know that in the deepest of his being that there is a scent, a subtle comforting knowing, that he was loved.

June 26

William and I hit another few rummage sales this morning. It's fun to go with him because he gets so excited about it. He searches the basement floor and the car for loose change and then he fills the drink coaster in the car with whatever he finds. Today, as I was doing the laundry, two dollars fell out of Sean's jeans pocket and I told William that Dad probably wouldn't mind if he used it, but William said, "No. Dad doesn't like it when we bring more junk into the house. It's not right to use his money on things he doesn't like." He folded the dollars neatly and laid them on Sean's dresser. That just goes to prove how much William is Sean's son.

We have a rummage ritual now. We each bring a cold drink along and then take a sip for luck before stepping out of the car. As we get closer to the signs, he says, "It's going to be a good one; I can feel it." William gathers his change and, each time, I count it out for him. He has become quite the negotiator. Today, he asked one woman if she would mind taking forty-seven cents instead of fifty for a Santa statue. We never spend much money, a dollar or two total (always less than a Starbucks coffee), but it has become a really special time for just the two of us and he is getting a little taste of what it might be like to be an only child. It is fun to watch him work up the courage to ask people, "How much would you like for this?" It is remarkable for me to watch because two years ago, he never would even look at someone he wasn't familiar with; he spent the first two years of school with his hand over his face most of the time.

He is supposed to be in bed now, but it is so hot in the house. He just came down to tell me that he has been watching the fireflies from his bedroom window. If he promises to put his shoes on, can he catch "just one? Please?' So there he is now, out in the summer dark, wearing winter flannel (but unbuttoned) doggie pajamas, catching lightning bugs. Last summer, he caught one and named it "Who." He released it on the front porch and said, "Goodbye, Who." He is the best at naming things. He had a fish called Bullet awhile back. Bullet died, I think, because our house was warm enough to poach him.

Today we found Bullet's former tank and filled it with water to prepare the Scooby Doo Chia Pet Head that William bought for a quarter. It was good for the fish tank to have a new and useful purpose. Born again. Tomorrow we will take Scooby out of the tank and paint it with the seeds that are germinating high up on the kid's bookshelf. Trash in to treasure, undoubtedly.

June 27

It is after midnight and we are all just getting home from my parents' house. The mosquitoes are out in full force; about four of them made their way into our car before we could shut the doors. They attacked us all the way home (everyone but Sean, mosquitoes don't like him; he says it's because he doesn't sweat) and we took turns swearing and slapping at them, while William kept wailing, "Don't kill them! They are living creatures." I told Sean that the thirty-minute ride was all the evidence that I needed to decide that we should never, ever go camping.

I think camping is a terrible invention anyway. When we were in college, I enrolled in a course called *Shamanism and Native American History*. I only took the course because Sean was in it, but then he dropped it and I was stuck there. The class took a weekend trip to the Delaware River Gap to build a sweat lodge and go camping. I didn't bring anything with me. We stopped at a grocery store on the way there and I had no idea what to buy. I ended up getting a bagel and some cream cheese, which ultimately soured and gave me food poisoning. We had to go on a nature hike when we were there, and our teacher showed us how to pick fiddleheads and eat them. These made me throw up as well (my naked teacher offered me some toilet paper. "I was saving it for myself, but here, you can have it," he sighed, as I threw up on a tree). The green tree buds also didn't sit well with another girl from the Midwest. She was smart enough to go to sleep; I stuck out the sweat lodge.

The memory of the sweat lodge itself feels like a dream. Most people were naked and they beat on drums while chanting the lyrics, "eagles in the sky-y, circling the universe," over and over. I sat across from a girl from my Critical Inquiry class. It was the second time in a week I had seen her topless. The first time was during a performance art piece in which she sat (topless) on the instructor's desk and played a looped cassette tape sounding "nice tits," over and over again. That's art school for you.

After the sweat lodge, it was time to sleep. There were about four of us who didn't bring anything along to sleep in. We shared a heavy plastic tarp, which one of the guys kept farting under and then repeatedly saying, "Oops, sorry. That was me." In the middle of the night, I walked to the woods to pee and ended up wetting my only pair of socks. In the morning, all the seasoned campers got out their little stoves and made pancakes. They did not share.

I returned to New York, sunburned and full of mosquito bites, the "eagle" lyrics stuck in my head. I have not slept outside since.

June 28

Today my dad couldn't reach my mom on her cell phone and it was driving him crazy. I asked if he left her a voicemail message, to which he replied, "I'd have better luck throwing a bottle into the ocean."

It's true. She does not check her messages. She does not keep a calendar either. All of her dates are up in her head somewhere. When I was little and we lived on 49th street, we had a calendar above the microwave cart. It had pictures of very colorful and realistic fruits and vegetables on every page. I think that it must have been the only calendar that my family ever had; otherwise I don't think I would remember such a thing. Either that, or we kept it hanging up for years. I loved it, though. I'd flip through its pages and stare at the ruby red beets or the asparagus dripping with water droplets.

My childhood friend Melissa lived with her mother in an apartment. I thought that it was very cool to have an apartment. They had a calendar of the sexiest firemen of 1980. July was not wearing pants. We would look at his white butt and giggle. Her mom had all sorts of things my mom did not have: a make up mirror with all the movie star bulbs, a closet full of high heels, nail polish. Her mom emphasized manners and drinking milk and the amount of minutes one should brush her teeth. Everything in their apartment was tan and beige.

Melissa spent each day with me in the summer while her mom was at work. We would spend hours playing "secretary," taking pretend phone calls for pretend doctors. I remember her mom not wanting her to play secretary. "Why not the doctor?"

she asked sharply. It was hard to explain then, but the joy of that game was not the part where we worked "for someone else." The gratifying part for me was making the telephone messages, the charts, the graphs, neatly penciling in dates. It was the beginning of my love for list making.

Once, in the beginning of our relationship, I unintentionally offended Sean by making a list about us. I don't remember the details of the list, but I remember him being upset. Now, when I make lists, like grocery lists, he always sneaks something into the list that surprises me later. Sometimes, I will be at the store reading "Tide, grapes, coffee, penile implant." Stuff like that. He gets me every time. I like my lists being interrupted.

I look forward every summer to when the new school calendar comes in the mail. I spend hours filling in the already known events into the virgin grid. It is not that I would forget Luke's birthday or what day Christmas is. Calendars and lists are not about remembering for me. This is why I still frequently forget "snack day." It is why I sent four-year-old Luke to school dressed as a spider for nursery rhyme character day on the wrong day. The joy is not in the remembering (though that would be nice). The joy is in the anticipation, in the plan. It is about eagerness and wishing.

June 29

Elizabeth woke up in the middle of the night again with bad dreams. I had taken Tylenol PM before I went to sleep so I was in a huge daze when she woke up screaming. I still don't remember what it was about; I only remember waking up as it was starting to get light out, curled around both kids in the lower bunk bed. Luke never had dreams like that. I did though; still do.

A few months ago I dreamt that I was walking in a tall field, holding William's hand. I looked down only to realize that we were not walking on ground, we were walking on alligator heads. I turned around to warn Luke and Elizabeth to turn around, but as I started to shout, they were sucked under, disappearing forever. I woke up, sucking in my breath.

Nothing terrifies me more than thoughts of my children disappearing. When Christopher, my brother, and I were little, he wandered into the elevator at Boston Store and the doors closed before my mom could get him. I remember racing with her to the escalator, not knowing if he went up or down. What's strange is that I don't remember finding him. I only remember my mom's panic.

My mom stayed home with me until I was five or six. I have lots of good memories from that time, but I also distinctly remember her panicking over things that happened to my brother, like the time he swallowed lots of cayenne pepper or the time that he sliced his head open when he ran into a door hinge. My mom ran in circles saying, "Call your dad. Call your dad." Once we waited in the emergency room while my doctors relocated my brother's dislocated arm. We could hear his screams, and my mom was white with anxiety and fear. I only understood her panic after I became a mother myself. At the time, I was just a curious observer.

Even now, I don't panic as much as Sean does. Yesterday Lizzie accidentally stabbed William in the leg with a scissors. She was using them to pop a balloon while he was kicking it. Sean scooped up William like a fireman hero and washed out the wound. Sean's energy gets really intense at moments like that. I am a little bit more like a deer in headlights. I need to pause. It was the same way when the dog ran off with a box of Chinese food and William yanked it back, causing the wire handle to pierce his eyebrow. Sean had William in the truck racing to the ER before I even digested what had taken place.

I think that is why Lizzie and I have vivid dreams. We take things in slowly, digesting not just the details, but the mood as well. Once Christopher said, "slowness takes time." I think that in that time, in the gap between stimulus and response, imaginations form, characters build, stories happen.

June 30

Midnight.

June is officially over. William will go to school for four weeks prior to its official start. He has done this for the last three summers, but this time he isn't looking forward to it. He is worried about missing prime rummage sale hours. I told him not to worry because we still have two more weeks.

I am trying to get so much done in one day. Today, all before 11 a.m., William and I had taken the car for an emissions test, registered the car, went to the post office, mailed bills, grocery shopped, watered the flowers, and washed the car. I even scrubbed the floor mats. After lunch, I mowed the lawn, repotted some dying plants to new shadier spaces, did the laundry, and made three puppets for Lizzie and her girlfriends. Sean and I grilled lots of food for dinner, even though the younger kids were out at sleepovers.

Being relatively kid free, I decided to take Luke to Target after dinner. About thirty minutes into our trip, the day caught up with me. I couldn't walk. Everything hurt. It was only nine o'clock. So often it feels like my mind and my desires are ten miles ahead of my body. I think that the radioactive iodine I took in 1997 really did poison me. Sometimes it feels like I am a human voodoo doll because the pain comes on suddenly. It feels almost like I would imagine getting caught in quicksand might, a sinking loss of mobility. Most of the time, the pain doesn't bother me anymore. Reiki is helping. This time, though, it was so frustrating. I just wanted to spend some time with Luke. He was looking forward to being alone, just the two of us. He brought his money along to maybe purchase a new PS3 game. We had to leave though. I couldn't even lift the two-dozen bottles of water I purchased.

I watched Julia Roberts on David Letterman tonight. He asked her if she ever took her kids to McDonald's. She said no twice. The second no was an, "Are you crazy, of course not!" no. Maybe that is what is wrong with me. I once babysat for a family in New York who bought organic everything. Their children had never even tasted sugar. So maybe I should be living more like that, more like Julia. I believe we are the same age.

I don't think so though. I think that I will be able to find value in what is happening to me. It must serve some purpose, or maybe the fact that I even believe there is one, is why the pain continues to stay. Maybe instead of my "shoulds," I can just give up the idea that there is a lesson in all of this. Maybe that is what the real me is waiting for, just the permission to let go and move on.

If that is what it is, I give myself permission as we all move into July.

July 1

Here's hoping the Allen wrench burns in hell. I know it's a handy little thing and, in the end, I was glad to have it, but damn that IKEA.

I bought a chair for Luke's desk, which was very easy to assemble. Ten minutes, done. I also bought a chaise lounge for the deck because it was marked way down and it was oh-so-lovely. When I first took it out of the box, I sighed a big breath of relief and said, "Oh, this will be okay, it's just the two wheels that need to go on," and then the bag with all the hardware fell out, to which I exclaimed, "Oh, fuck!" The one good thing about IKEA directions is that there aren't any words, just pictures. Unfortunately, I did not see that in one of the pictures that two of the four legs that looked identical were really different, in that two of them had a tiny little hole on the left. An hour later, I disassembled my mistake and started over again. In this case it would have been helpful to have words that read, "Two of these things are not like the others." Initially, I had considered buying two of these chairs (they were that cheap), but talked myself out of it. Next time I go to IKEA, I am going to wear a tee shirt that reads, "Four Thousand Tiny Parts," or maybe it will just be a picture of myself jamming an Allen wrench into my eye socket.

July 2

Pharaoh day. Luke took my breath away. His performance filled me up. I sat next to Sean who was so nervous that his hand clenched mine immediately before Luke make his grand entrance. He proceeded to laugh and cry at the same time while our darling boy proved to the world (or at least to the 120 people in the Montessori gym) what it means to have stage presence.

When Luke was born he weighed two pounds, six ounces. My dad got to see him hours before I did and when he described him to me he said that his head was smaller than an orange. Since that April twelve years ago, I have continued to love a boy who generates peace. Today, I was his proud fan. I felt the way I know William felt when he learned to ride his bike last month, just bursting with terrific, unabashed joy.

After the show, lots of other parents congratulated Luke and told Sean and me over and over again how impressed they were. This was all very nice, but what I couldn't really explain to anyone was that they were witnessing a life take off in a way that started off with such fragility.

Those of us in the audience who knew Luke back then, who had once felt the entire span of his delicate back resting gently across four fingers, understood why Sean cried. It was more than pride and excitement. It was a release.

July 3

Elizabeth hates her eyebrows. This saddens me: that she has reached the age at which she has begun to dissect her features and hunt for flaws. She has beautiful moon shaped eyebrows that frame the bluest of eyes, but she doesn't like the way they move when she talks. This is what sleeping over at a girlfriend's house can do.

I distinctly remember riding in the way back of a station wagon with four other girls on my way to a sleepover. I was nine or ten and we were playing a game. Each of us had to take a turn naming the one feature that we didn't like on the other girls. All the girls in the car chose my nose. I wish that the mom who had been driving that car had pulled over to the side of the road and cupped our individual faces between her palms and told each of us that we were beautiful girls and that each feature played a role in building our unique looks and that eyebrows move to give us expression. She didn't say anything though and I remember, even then, wishing she'd stop the game, not wanting to choose, not knowing which feature to pick on my friend's face. This is how women's magazines are born.

I also know what the mom in the car knew. Nothing I can say to Elizabeth will eliminate her doubt completely. I can gush all over her all that I want to, but she will resist. So instead I told her about a girl I went to college with who also hated her eyebrows, but it was very stupid of her to hate them because she shaved them off and then for the rest of her life people who normally wouldn't have paid any attention at all to her eyebrows ended up staring at the spaces where they used to be and wonder about what had happened to them. Elizabeth thought this was very funny and that the girl was a fool. Then she told me that she once had a substitute teacher who only had half of an eyebrow. We concluded that it was best to have regular old eyebrows that move.

July 4

For most of my life, my family went down to the lakefront to watch the fireworks on July 3rd. I don't know why Milwaukee does this on the third and not the fourth, but regardless, it's an amazing fireworks display. We stopped going a few years ago, I think when Sean first hurt his back or maybe it was when I hurt my foot or maybe it was when Lolo decided she was too old to go anymore. My dad took William to the art museum (which also happens to be along the lakefront) a few weeks ago and was horrified to learn that William didn't remember seeing the fireworks there. My dad and I agreed that this was criminal.

Yet we didn't go again this year. Sean and my dad both had to work and Lizzie had a doctor's appointment to re-X-ray her broken wrist. My feet and ankles were swollen to the size of grapefruits (I guess from the humidity) and Sean got a speeding ticket, so no one was really in the mood to go. That's the thing about being the caboose kid; everyone loses any sense of urgency, or maybe, we just understand that there is more than one way to skin a cat/raise a kid.

What William did remember about the Fourth of July was going to our friend, Cathy's house and watching her neighbors' fireworks display from the driveway. Last year, we did this and the kids played a game called, "Hey, get off my lawn," which from the outside, anyway, appears to be tag. I asked William why they didn't ever play that game at our house and he said, "Lawn's not big enough. We can only do it at Cathy's."

So we went over there, lit sparklers, and sat, lined up in chairs along the dark driveway to watch the show while the kids chased each other in the vast lawn. It's no lakefront, but there is no trouble parking, no long walk back to the car, no sore feet, and the kids are just as happy.

Every year on the Fourth, at least one of my parents has to tell the story of what I said the first year I saw fireworks. This year it was my mom. I had just learned my animal sounds, and when the grand finale lit up the sky, instead of repeating, "Boom, boom!" as I had been doing throughout the display, I gushed, "Oh, Moo!" I have now heard this story thirty-six times.

I guess that is the important part: ritual. Repetition: the weaving of memory. I am pretty sure that years from now, William will have heard over and over again, how on one Fourth of July we wore his plaid shorts to match his dad and his blue polo shirt to match his grandpa and that he ran, sparkler in hand, playing a game called, "Hey, GET OFF MY LAWN!"

July 5

I was inspired by Cathy to clean out my closet. This might have been a mistake, as my closet is kind of like a tomb. I open the door and the world falls out. Ugh. Determined to have this summer be a fresh start, I dove in. I even took my wedding dress out.

About twenty minutes in I started to wheeze from all of the dust. I plowed on, even painting the walls. I went to the store and bought closet organizers and had visions of my closet looking like something out of *Real Simple.*

I started this whole project around eleven this morning. It is after midnight now and I'm still not done. I have boxes and boxes of old letters, photos, and sketchbooks, and piles of clothes that don't fit me anymore (but one day might), pay stubs from ten years ago, including a receipt for our rent on Homer Street (three babies ago), crutches, paintings, slides from college, notes from Susie in seventh grade. I know that I should throw most of it out. I should edit. I'm really not a packrat. I usually toss stuff. It's just all this little stuff that has built up. I really don't want to throw the letters out because I have this fear that one day I will be really old and by myself with nothing to do and I can read these letters when I am feeling nostalgic and tell my grandchildren that I lived during a time when email did not exist and people actually sent thoughts via post. Either that, or I will die and my grown children will find these letters and they will read them and giggle about the person I once was. Just like in *Bridges of Madison County*, except that I won't have had an affair with Clint Eastwood. In fact, nothing in my memoirs is even close to that scandalous.

Yet I don't know where to put it all. My closet is only big enough for clothes. A year ago, I made one of those visionary boards about where I wanted my life to be one day. One of the things that I cut out was a little sentence from *Dwell* magazine that read, "Expand my space." I hear that sentence in my head a lot. I even say it out loud when I am driving and I feel that other drivers aren't giving me enough room. If I were to make a visionary board today, I would head the entire thing with just that theme: more space.

Until that space shows up though, I will sit on the floor, surrounded by pieces of me, wondering how to shelve and preserve a life; wonder if it's worth preserving and if it matters whether or not it fits into shoe towers and high-end milk crates. The only thing I've learned for sure in the last twelve hours is that it's not real simple.

July 6

Still wheezing.

Squirrelly kids, too-hot house, dust in my lungs, and a bad game of tag involving a large beanbag weapon.

I spent a half an hour this afternoon trying to dig out a quarter from Elizabeth's cast. She used it to scratch an itch. The doctors told her not to use Q-tips or hangers, but they didn't say anything about pocket change. I was in her room, still sorting the closet mess when I heard, "Uh oh." Ironically, I had to use a coat hanger to get it out.

That's pretty much how the rest of the day went.

July 7

No one slept well last night. The humidity was like a thick milkshake; we could literally suck it in. We had the upstairs window units on, but the air was still heavy and still, waiting for a storm. As soon as I'd drift off, one kid or the other would wake up to tell me that they could not sleep.

I woke up very early, while they were still in bed, and went to school to do some work. It was nice to be up early, being productive while everyone at home slept in. I met with the agency and gave them new work for the 2009 holiday season. They liked it and wanted to see more by Wednesday, so I ended up drawing all day: ghosts, cats, elves, and a lot of reindeer. Lizzie watched me work. She sat next to me and pulled work out of the printer when it was done. She did this for hours, always having a comment or a suggestion of what I should add or do. I told her I didn't know what to do for Hanukah, but she said, "That thing with the eight sticks," so I guess I'll start menorahs tomorrow. At the end of the night, she said, "I just want to tell you that I am so excited for you and I know you worked really hard on all these drawings. It's a lot of work." She was grinning sweetly, all lit up, proud.

I was reminded of the e.e. cummings poem that hung on Luke's incubator for three months and was later read at our wedding. I looked at Elizabeth and wondered silently, "I don't know what it is about you that opens and closes; only something in me understands the voice of your eyes is deeper than all roses." She is so deep under my skin that I can feel her when I sleep. Even though there are days like yesterday (quarters dropping, beanbags swinging into crying bodies, constant complaining), I am still awed by how intensely I love these kids and humbled by how much they love me back.

July 8

I was saddened to realize that I missed the anniversary of bringing Luke home from the hospital. It was July 5th. This is the first year I've forgotten. St. Joe's recommended that I stay on the eighth floor for a few nights with him before actually taking him home, as all he had known for nine weeks, was the incubator. I eagerly agreed, but found myself in full shock at what it was like actually to be with a tiny four-pound baby all night long. He cried endlessly and loudly, horrible, tortuous screams, and he was hooked up to a monitor twice his size. That monitor recorded that he had stopped breathing seventeen times overnight only the week before. The screaming continued for my entire stay. The soft, padded nurses would come in and try to teach me, to help me, but I was resentful of them. They were too damn calm, which I took to be condescending. I thought I should just intuitively know what to do, but outside the safety of the pristine N.I.C.U with the comforting smell of that pink, foamy antibacterial soap, I was lost. In retrospect, I don't know why Sean didn't stay with me or why the hospital didn't invite him to do so.

I wonder if much of life ends up like that: we live awhile and then look back and wonder why in the world we did "it" like that. Does anyone look back and feel really proud? Sure footed? Not of the big moments, but of the ordinary day to day?

Today, I lived outside of myself, procrastinated cleaning my mess of a bedroom. I did not draw menorahs. I don't even know what I did, really. I did spend about fifteen minutes thinking about Pringles and how whoever invented stacking chips up into a perfect cylinder was a genius. I sat on the leather chair, lining up their perfect salty curve to match the curve of my tongue. The other day I bought ten cans of them and when Sean came home he said, "Jesus, what did you do, buy stock in Pringles?"

This is exactly what I mean. In a few months, it will be freezing and snowy outside. Will I get there and then wonder what I did with my summer and fill myself with regret about how I should have lived? If I am staring at processed potatoes that come in fourteen different flavors, kicking myself for missing a milestone anniversary, am I not noticing something else that is very important, very obvious, and just lost on me? It seems, maybe, like a waste of a thought, but when I look back on that first week of July more than a decade ago, I find myself wishing that I had known myself more, and I'm pretty sure that there is more that I could be doing to know myself better right now.

I don't know what that "more" is, however; so in the meantime, happy belated anniversary, dear, sweet Luke. I am sorry that I was so nervous around you in the beginning. Forgive me. I know more now.

July 9

Sean, Susie, and I went to a cute rooftop patio Irish restaurant for dinner, and I found myself talked into ordering bangers and mash, which was very unlike me. We had fun and laughed a lot. Sean was very excited to know that they served hot homemade doughnuts for dessert. Susie and I wanted to go to the casino afterwards. Sean went back home, as he doesn't have any tolerance for slot machines. He says he might as well feed money to a goat. He says the same thing, however, whenever I hang potted plants on the front porch ("Might as well hang twenty dollar bills out there, because those are going to die in about a week.").

He was right. It was a waste of our time and money. Plus, everyone at that place looks like they just arrived from some dilapidated bus terminal. It was so smoky that my contact lenses fogged over and didn't sit right in my eyes after fifteen minutes of being there. The entire place smelled like a combination of ashtrays, silly putty, butt crack, and those stick on air fresheners that we all used in our sixth grade lockers. That smell just gets recycled through the vents and pretty soon we both felt like we had been living in some moldy basement.

It's so deceiving from the outside, with its neon promise of glamour and excitement. One can imagine Willy Wonka, showgirls, maybe even a Disney character or two inside, greeting us with little cakes and tiny tea sandwiches. The only people there to greet us were bored security men, bathed in beige and brown, eyes glazed over, staring straight ahead. I wonder if the casino ever shuts down for a day and just lets the security guards go nuts in there, free tokens all around.

In the long run, I would have preferred to spend the money on another round of drinks at dinner, enjoying the roof garden, saying hello to the dogs that came to visit, laughing with my best friends. And probably, I would have even preferred feeding the money to a goat.

July 10

I went to UPS today to mail the invitations to my mom's art show next month. While there, an African American grandmother and her two small grandchildren walked in. She asked, "Do you have any of that brown paper that comes in a roll? See, we want to lay her down on it and trace her." She pointed to the young girl who was about five. The clerk said no. She insisted, "Yes you *do*. You know, that brown paper? You use it to wrap packages in all the time. I know you have to have it. I don't want to go into Walgreens. It will take me forever and a day to get out of Walgreen's with these two."

The clerk explained that they no longer wrap packages like that because the paper tends to rip. The grandmother said, "I bet you have *white* paper." The word white came out like spit. She looked at me. I knew she was thinking that it would be easier to have to color in brown on white paper than it would be to put two kids back in the car and try another store. She was also thinking that it wasn't the first time she'd have to compromise for something white.

I liked her immediately because I could so identify with not wanting to go into a drug store with two little ones. It was at that same Walgreens where I dragged out a three-year-old Luke after he tipped over an entire shelf of deodorant because I said no to a candy request. I picked him up and cradled him under my arm, his body a stiff cardboard cutout, and he screamed, repeatedly, "I hate you. I hate you. You are a stupid mother. A stupid, stupid mother."

Though my transaction was long over at UPS, I was frozen at the counter, watching this interaction. I so wanted to help. I wanted to be able to say, "Know what? I have some Kraft paper right in my trunk. Let me go grab it," or at the very least be able to suggest a nearby store that wouldn't be so inviting to a pre-school child. My mind didn't move though. I couldn't stop myself for staring. I even followed them out once the UPS college student convinced her that they didn't have *any* paper, not even the white kind.

They walked down the sidewalk, through the parking lot towards Walgreens. The girl said, "Granny, this is so boring!" As they made their way away from my stalking eyes, Granny said, "I'm not here to entertain you. I am here to watch over you. You gotta *pay* for entertainment," and I liked her even more.

July 11

I slipped on a piece of spinach at the grocery store tonight. I went flying and twisted my ankle. The spinach streaked across the floor and looked like a stain on a diaper. The manager came over and took all my information. He was very nice, though he gave a finger shake to the young boy in charge of the produce department, which I found to be slightly embarrassing for us both. I have a skinned knee now. Silly. If there is a heaven and my Grandma Jean was watching, she would have wet her angel pants laughing at the whole thing. Had she been with me, she would have giggled all the way home.

I think, sometimes, that moments like that are predestined. I almost went to the other grocery store; in fact, I was headed in that direction. I changed my mind because even though the other one is cheaper, it's grungy and poorly designed; I can never find anything in there. So at the last minute, I went to the store on State Street instead. I had to wait at the hot food case for awhile. I wonder if it was all in the timing. If I hadn't stopped to get baked hot cod, if I had grown impatient waiting, if I stopped to bag plums, would I have still fallen? Is that really just chance? I can't believe that.

In fact, I know it has something to do with the cosmos reinforcing my core belief, the one that's been drilled into me since I was five years old, that "thoughts are things and they create." I had *just* been thinking that I hoped nothing terrible happened before our trip to Vegas next month, like, I said to myself, "spraining my ankle." I take this spill as a warning to shield myself from thoughts like this. I will now officially declare that NOTHING bad is going to happen before, during, or after, our vacation. My feet will be in good working order and all my parts will be whole. Create that.

This is not what I was going to write about today. I was going to write about my continued and growing regret and resentment that Julia Roberts has not fed her children so much as a fast food french fry (we went to McDonald's twice this week). I was also going to write about my new discovery: a lotion called *Chub Rub*, for fat thigh chafing. A prayer heard and answered, for sure.

Nonetheless, I felt compelled to honor the grocery store fall because I believe that little piece of spinach heard my fear and was generous enough to warn me with just a tiny sprain; just enough of a warning to get me to stop worrying. I am also fully relieved to have had the wherewithal to keep this thought "on the inside," as I gave my personal information to the manager, who did not need to know that a part of me believes that spinach can hear.

July 12

While I was flat ironing my hair tonight, I watched E!'s *Best and Worst Beach Bodies report*. Pamela Anderson made it to number one. Go Pam. I was extremely irritated though when the panel kept going on and on about Beyonce's curves. "She's got real woman curves," they said four hundred times. I could fit all of Beyonce in the right leg of my jeans.

I both hate and adore entertainment television. I know I should ban it. I should be morally opposed to it, but I occasionally still find myself caught up in its false luxury. It is the same reason I like to read magazines. It always cracks me up to read magazines about "the office," or to see those pie charts that divide up how much money women spend on clothes, the spa, "dining out". Food is always like 2% and "hair" is at around 50%. I don't know any of these women, women, who have desks and office parties with cakes, wear seasonal suiting, get weekly massages, and pay to get their hair blown out every Monday. The flip side is to read magazines about Jell-O recipes and "how to get stains out of the family room," so I guess that's how I end up reading *People* or *InStyle*. As long as I don't relate to the women anyway, they might as well be of the famous variety.

I am thinking about inventing some kind of human shock collar that kicks in each time I distract myself with useless information. We are a country at war, after all. I know more today about Girard Depardieu's cellulite (number two on the worst beach body list) than I do about anything happening in Iraq, Afghanistan, or even New Orleans for that matter. I can tell you who sang and what was eaten at Nelson Mandela's ninetieth birthday party. I can tell you all about the window treatment that was painted over Angelina Jolie's hospital delivery room to ensure her privacy. Britney Spears is on tour with Madonna, her sister Jaime Lynn had a girl. Toby Maguire flipped out over paparazzi today because their bulbs were blinding him. Jennifer Aniston has hooked up with John Mayer, nine years her junior, and Gwyneth Paltrow wore a fantastic peek-a-book Stella McCartney dress to the event she attended this month with B.F.F. Liv Tyler (who, by the way, didn't even know that her dad was Steven Tyler until she was like nine).

People were abused today, angry, starved, mistreated, disposed of. I am getting the shock collar, or at the very least, will consider yoga as a replacement to Ryan Seacrest.

July 13

We went to see *Hellboy II* tonight. It was fantastic and especially exciting to see because we got to look for our friend Fred's name in the credits. Luke spotted his name first. When I was cleaning out my closet last month I found my high school yearbook and it flipped open to my brother's page. Fred is in the same row. I was shocked to see how young they both were, boys, really, two years older than Luke is now.

One of my favorite stories about high school-Fred is the one where his mom, Marion, insisted that he come to her office downtown to type his paper, as it was already late and he was in the habit of procrastinating such things. He took the bus all the way down there, but forgot the paper. She told him "too bad," and that he'd have to take the bus back home and get it, which he did. He took the bus back home and then all the way back to Marion's downtown office again only to realize that he *still* forgot the paper.

So it is always rewarding, and a relief to his mom, I'm sure, that his name now flashes across the Ultra Screen; proof to the whole world that he's doing what he loves to do, what he always loved to do, and that sometimes, term papers are just excuses for gathering other ideas while riding the bus.

I also find a bit of solace in knowing that Fred has done well for himself, as Luke, too, often gets lost in the right side of his brain. Like the time I was shopping for Christmas gifts and was having such luck that I told Luke to go grab a cart. He came back a full thirty minutes later with someone else's full cart. He said that I didn't say to find an empty one. I wasn't "pacific," he said.

He will fall into his own, I'm sure, whether or not I am specific. Like Hellboy's girlfriend Liz says when worried about Hellboy's future, "I'll deal with it." She knows that whatever comes up, no struggle can hold a candle to loving someone who is so magnificent.

July 14

I dropped Luke and his friend off at the Marquette basketball camp this morning. There must have been five hundred boys there, all in yellow jerseys, shooting balls as music blared from the speakers. I was overwhelmed at first and Lizzie said the place scared her. I stayed for a few minutes to make sure the boys were comfortable and okay. I was good enough not to shout out, "Goodbye, sweet Luke! Farewell! Come give me a kiss, darling!" An exaggeration, I know, but still hard to just walk away silently. I did notice that within the first minute or two one of the coaches blew his whistle at Luke and told him to do five push-ups (for an air ball, whatever that is). My heart sank a little at that, wanting to run up to that man and explain that Luke just got there and didn't know the rules yet. I watched Luke laugh it off, drop down and give him five. It was in that moment that I first understood why Sean is hard on Luke sometimes, why men, in general, don't want their boys to be fragile or too sensitive. There is a world out there that I just don't get and it involves whistles and buzzers.

When Lizzie and I left and walked towards the parking lot, a woman told her, "You have the most gorgeous hair I have ever seen." She smiled and said thank you. Usually, Elizabeth tires of people saying things like this, but I could tell that she felt relief in knowing that someone not only noticed her, but that she stood out against that sea of boys. She didn't belong there and didn't want to belong there. I asked her how she wanted to spend our morning, just the two of us, a girl day at long last. She said, without pausing, "Lets go to the spa." I loved that, even though we did not go to a spa of any kind.

We did share an egg sandwich at Alterra and went shopping. We tried on clothes in the dressing room at Old Navy and she told me that polka dots weren't my style. She asked that her purchases be bagged separately and she held that bag, along with my purse, my sunglasses pushed back along her hairline, down the length of the mall.

I love the boys. They cuddle and need me. They are fun to have around. They make me laugh, and they hold my heart in the most delicate way possible, but there is something about having a daughter that makes me breathe easy. There is "a little me" out there. She'll do it better than I did, and that's okay. I won't have to blow any whistles to make it happen.

July 15

I saw Martina today, for more energy work. I am intent on changing my belief patterns, ones that were set too long ago for no real reason at all. For example, she asked me what my first thoughts were when I fell at the grocery store. I told her that I thought, "Of course, I fell." She asked me what would happen if instead of reinforcing the doubt about myself, I instead said something like, "Wow. I have an amazing body. Nothing broke!" It's a subtle difference, but for someone like me who deep down believes that she is clumsy and stagnant, it's a significant difference.

She had me close my eyes and try to remember the first time I felt scared of my body and I flashed back to swimming in the Missouri college pool with my dad. I was practicing swimming. He would stand a few yards away and I would swim to him. One time, though, he backed up without telling me and I panicked. I was scared and angry and I felt tricked. Martina asked me why my dad backed up. I told her that he backed up because he thought I could make it. He believed I could go further. She asked what if I had recognized that then. What if I had, instead of giving into fear, thought, "My dad believes I can do this. That's so exciting." She had me close my eyes again and imagine being back in that pool, except this time, she had me swim all the way to him. She asked how I felt, doing that. I had to admit I felt proud of myself.

It was an important exercise for me because it helped me notice how powerful choosing is. I have always been able to ask "What else? What If?" when it comes to making decisions about words or images, stories or paintings. I guess I forgot to apply that same idea to my everyday thinking.

I like that Martina gives me really specific imagery to work with. I can visualize change in my body and spirit. Today she told me to stop digging up my own seed. She meant, she said, that because I have been struggling for so long, she senses my impatience, but she warned: Once you plant a seed, you can't dig it up all the time because it just won't grow. She said thoughts like the one I had at the grocery store are weeds. Weed the garden and water the seed and be willing to be patient. This might sound silly, which is fine. All that matters, really, is that I can see a tiny little watering can above a Dixie cup filled with potting soil and so much depends on that image. Today, I learned that I can be the gardener.

July 16

When I was a kid I loved getting school supplies. I particularly enjoyed picking out my Trapper Keeper. That is a great name: Trapper Keeper. It is like a movie star's first born. (Side note: Nicole Kidman just named her baby Sunday Rose. Kim commented that she had given birth to an American Girl doll. I told my mom that Angelina Jolie just named her son Knox and she asked, "as in Fort?"). That decides it. If I am ever famous and ever decide to breed yet another time, I will name that child Trapper Keeper, reminiscent of sixth grade, Sr. Florence, and Trapper John, M.D. (for my twelfth birthday my friend gave me a poster of Trapper John, shirtless. My dad was mortified).

Anyway, I'd always stack up my new supplies in a tidy pile next to my bed and carefully write my name on the inside of everything. I'd practice making my capital F the way my mom makes hers. In college, I used my Grandma Jean's F. Now I just have my own.

Today, I have the choice of paying my kid's school $180 to buy supplies for all three of them or just try to wing it on my own. I choose to do it because I love looking at all of the rows of neatly stacked notebooks, glue sticks, markers. The thing is, it's not the same today. We used to be able to pick whatever colors we wanted. If I wanted a folder decorated with horses, it was not a problem. Transformers? Fine. Hello Kitty? Copasetic. Now the lists my kids get do not only say (I am NOT kidding) "No Trapper Keepers." They also tell me exactly what color notebooks to buy. This includes grey. Does anyone know how difficult it is to find a grey notebook? I'd have an easier time finding a John Travolta notebook.

I went to three stores today. Three. I still cannot find Glue Dots. Apparently, kids in the new millennium do not get to experience the joy of peeling Elmer's glue from their hands after making dioramas of Ancient Greece. These days, they just use a conveniently sized "dot." Not too much, not too little. Where is the joy in that? They will never know the satisfaction gained from using a paper clip to unclog the sticky bottle. I also cannot find pink ("or red," it says) pencil top erasers. The list *specifically* says, "Not assorted colors." I asked Elizabeth why this was the case, and she said it was because last year kids fought over the colors.

That's the other thing. Everyone shares. That's bullshit. They don't even get to label their stuff and that is the best part! "These aren't your colored pencils. They are ours." A collective "We." Yuck. That's why they fight over the colors. If they had their own pack, it would not be an issue. They don't even get to buy pencil cases! That was always my favorite item. I loved the rubber ones shaped like giant pencils that opened at the "eraser." The smell of those things alone was intoxicating, however, in retrospect, probably not so good to inhale.

When Luke came home from basketball practice, I gave him a giant, stuffed white bag and said, "Luke! Here are your supplies for next year." He just shrugged and told me to set them "somewhere." He didn't even look inside the bag! Elizabeth was excited only about her backpack.

That settles it. I will just have to give birth to little Trapper. He will most certainly have the same affinity for notebooks that I do. If not, maybe his twin sister (Sharpie? Crayola? Ticonderoga?) will.

July 17

William was upset this morning because a boy in his summer class told him that God was the father of all of us. William got in the car and said that was the "stupidest" thing he had ever heard. I tried to explain it as a figure of speech and even told him about the Lord's Prayer. He didn't buy it and finally shouted (very loudly and red-faced), "MY FATHER IS SEAN MIZER!" I asked him what he said to the boy after the boy declared God as Father. William said, "I told him, 'Yeah, right. And Jesus is my mother." Luckily, this caught me so off guard, I did not laugh. Ay. I can imagine how that conversation will sound in the other kid's car.

William has found much of the world to be quite stupid lately. For example, tonight he read a book about mammals. He read that all mammals have fur or hair, but was then angry that the illustrator has a picture of a dolphin on that same page. "I don't see any hair on dolphins! Stupid!" When he read further that humans have hair (making them mammals), Will said with complete disgust, "Everyone knows that! Why bother writing that down?" I figure that he will do pretty well on the debate team one day. Either that or he'll be kicked off of it.

July 18

Happy Day-of-Birth. Patrick and Sativa had their third child, a girl, early this morning. Their six year old helped deliver her in the bathtub at home. She does not have a name yet; Pat said her face was still too puffy to name her.

I knew it was a girl. Grandma Jean (Patrick's mom) has been present in my life since she died. I don't know why. Maybe it is because she died next to me, because I was there at the exact moment her spirit left her body. She must have seen me laughing then because I was so stunned.

Her spirit woke me in the middle of the night last November. I was about half way asleep and the hummed lyrics "And He walked with me and He talked with me" from her memorial service played in my head. It woke me up. I opened my eyes but didn't see anything. I felt the words, "Hi, Love." She wanted to let me know how much she liked Lizzie's school picture and that she had seen the dollhouse that my parents bought her for Christmas. She said she had a dollhouse when she was young and that it was grayish-blue. She communicated a lot more stuff, and did say that someone would be having a baby soon and it would be a girl. I told Patrick that two weeks later at Thanksgiving and he went white, not having told anyone yet about Sativa's pregnancy.

When I saw Martina for the first time, she could actually see Grandma (purple light above my left shoulder). Even when Martina was doing the reiki my grandma kept bumping into her and laying yellow roses all over me. Martina said she kept saying repeating the words, "baby girl." I realized only just now that the lyrics "roses with dew" are in that same Jim Reeves song.

The other thing that she noted during her metaphysical visit was the song "Brown Eyed Girl." She played this in my head when I asked her who she was with, who greeted her when she died? I am guessing that my Grandpa used to sing that to her. I will also bet that this newest little addition has the biggest, deepest brown eyes that any of us have ever seen. They will be like chocolate caramels. Even though this is the only grandchild that my grandma never got to hold, I'm pretty sure that when I look into these eyes, I will be able to feel her arms wrapping tightly around all of us. *"And the joy we share as we tarry there none other has ever known."*

July 19

I invented a word today: Kabloom.

I went to the *Explorations with Mary* meeting in Brookfield today. Mary is a group of spirit guides channeled through a woman named Jacque. On my way there, I kept thinking about how Martina told me to stop "digging up my own seed."

At the beginning of the session, Don, Jacque's husband, was saying that he and Jacque would take sixteen people to Costa Rica in January. I looked down at the lid of my Alterra to-go cup and saw that the word "Traveler" was embossed on its lid.

Mary knows that I do not have patience for patience. They said that because what I want is so big and so involved, it might take a bit of time to grow that seed. Then they gave me great advice: Distract yourself. It seems like such an easy answer (Want the water to boil? Walk away). So now, when I experience those moments, when it feels like I'm waiting in an airport terminal, I will distract myself: garden, sew, mop the floors, teach.

Sometimes when Mary speaks, they make little firecracker sounds, little explosions of energy. "Pow, pow, pe-OW." Between Martina's seed metaphor and Mary's crackles, Kabloom appeared. It is a very good, distracting word. I imagine myself as a caped super hero: Negative thought? KaBLOOM! Self doubt? KaBLOOM. Impatience? KaBLOOOOOOM. If nothing else, I will use Kabloom to grow my "seeds." A garden of wishes fulfilled, blooming.

We are going to Costa Rica.

Kabloom.

July 20

Happy Birthday, Grandpa George. We sent him a hooded sweatshirt embroidered with a Jack Russell Terrier, good for cold nights on the boat and Sunday drives when the leaves start to change. When I spoke to him he said he'd been giving the dog almost empty jars of peanut butter because she licks them clean and watching the progression from sticky to spotless is pretty entertaining.

I have been teaching Elizabeth and William to remember the months of the year in order. I have a big cup of change on my dresser. Each time we name a month, I give them a coin for anything that they can name that takes place during that time. When we first started playing the game, I was shocked to realize that the only thing they could name (besides their own birthdays) was Greta's birthday. Not even Christmas made it. The dog trumped us all. We slowly progressed to things like "March . . . you know that thing with the leprechauns," to actually naming St. Patrick's Day.

Playing the game reminded me of the rhythm of our years, the something significant each month. I think that I spend a lot of time looking forward to something. Once, in high school, I went with my Meditation teacher to Milwaukee Zen and we had to sit for hours facing a white wall, trying not to think, trying just to be, while a Buddhist master held a ruler to our backs to straighten our spines. I can tell you right now that this method was not for me and that it was only one step up from being stuck in traffic or waiting in a doctor's office without magazines to read.

Though I appreciate the value of living in the moment, of enjoying now, I don't think I'll ever understand the point of doing that by staring blankly at nothing. I'd rather practice just "being" with a gin and tonic and a jar of olives, or maybe a nice lemon meringue pie. Plus, I like the anticipation of what is next: July, Grandpa George and William, August, Grandma Pat, September, Christopher, October, Lolo, November, Sean, December, Susie, January, Grandpa Greg, February, me and Love Day, March, Oma and the not-to-be-forgotten leprechauns, April, Luke and Grandma Barbara, May, Lizzie, June, Happy Anniversary. Start all over again.

It's not very Zen. Watching Scooter eat peanut butter is probably more so, but for now, I am content to practice the art of looking ahead instead.

July 21

Today I asked William if he wanted apples or fries with his drive-thru (sorry, Julia) kids meal. He said that it would be more interesting if the question was between apples and flies. I told him that it would make for an easier decision anyway.

Tomorrow he turns seven. On his last day of his sixth year, he caught the tiniest frog I have ever seen. Maybe that's where the flies comment came from. Maybe he wished he could feed that frog.

He put his grandpa to work today, as I had to go to their house to cook all the food for the party. He showed my dad where to put up the volleyball net, the kiddie pool, the slip and slide. It was as if he had orchestrated the entire event in his head several months ago.

He is a little bit apprehensive about going to school in the morning, mostly because he does not want to sing, "I am seven years old, I'm seven years old," in front of the class. In this way, he is very different from his brother, who would probably ask for a microphone and a spotlight (possibly even a costume). I don't really know that I am fully ready for him to be seven. It seems to mark the end of "little kid," and the start of "big kid." He wants to get his haircut like Luke's. I am not ready to lose his long blond little boy hair. It's funny because when Luke was little, I cried at all of his "firsts:" first day of school, first lost tooth, etc. I didn't do that with the other kids, but now I'm finding myself just a little nostalgic about the "lasts." No one follows the caboose.

Although it is not nearly as dramatic, and not at all devastating, it still feels a little like finding out one only has so many more months to live. He still lets me cuddle up around him when he is sleeping, scratch his back, comb his hair, talk about outer space and lightning bugs. I am still his whole world. Today his sister, just a year older, wanted to spend her first night without her cast celebrating at a friend's house. I am a sideliner for her now, a peripheral comfort. For me, seven is the last year that I get to be the headliner. He can't cut his hair just yet.

July 22

Happiest of all birthdays, sweet, sweet, William. Oh, ugh, saying that creates immediate lumps in my throat.

He woke up and sang "Happy Birthday to Me," in his boxer shorts, in front of his full-length mirror. He opened the presents from us. When I was little, my parents used to wake us up with breakfast in bed and tons of presents. Even if we had a kitchen, I don't think we'd do that. Somehow, that only works with two kids, four years apart. Once anyone adds that third kid, breakfast in bed is just a bad idea. We still do have presents right away in the morning though, to start the day off right and to spread things out a bit.

I don't know when it happened (I guess a number of years ago), but Sean and I always buy our gifts for the kids separately. Sean always wraps his in copper foil paper. He gets things like guns that shoot marshmallows, and soccer balls. I get stuffed dogs and panda backpacks. I used to hate this, that Sean would go out and buy his own presents, but now I look forward to it and I can understand why he, or anyone for that matter, would want to give a gift all by himself.

Here is what I know about William at seven: He loves the color yellow. He likes the way egg farts smell. He likes to collect things (bugs, bottle caps, Webkinz, quarters, key chains). His favorite foods are still donuts and pizza. He likes the candy machines by exit doors at restaurants and supermarkets, and he likes the word "cozy," and everything it implies: soft blankets, big overstuffed animals, nests, beds, pockets.

As I hugged him goodbye at school this morning, I knew that I understood something else about him. He has a worry that runs through him like a pulse. He understands, fully, that the "real" world will require him to do things (like go to school, start something new, maybe even sing a stupid song in front of practical strangers), and he is up for the challenge. He will do it, but he will do it with the prickly, bitter taste of anxiety at the back of his throat. There is not much I can do about that, except understand that it is a difficult way to live sometimes. And I can love him. I can do that for sure.

July 23

When I was about five or six my dad would play a game with me when it was time to go to bed. He'd scoop me up and put me in funny places, like the kitchen sink. "Is this your bed?" he'd ask. I would of course giggle and say no, until ultimately, he found my top bunk bed and I would say, "Yes, yes! This is the right one."

I love the ritual of going to bed. I love crawling underneath fresh sheets and allowing the day to collapse. I pushed our bed against the wall awhile back and I like feeling how cold the wall is against my legs. I like reading a magazine in my dimly lit room and I like thinking about tomorrow. Greta curls under my legs at the bottom of the bed, buried under all of the blankets, and she dreams. I know that I'll never be the kind of person that depends on methodical certainty. I am grateful to have surrounded myself, however, with people who do. That way, when I collapse into my sheets, I can be free to dwell in possibility.

Our friend, T, always wakes up at five in the morning because as a kid, that is what he'd do with his grandfather. Although I like the way morning feels I don't much like waking up in it. However, I understand the drive behind T's routine. It is all about the comforts of ritual.

Sean has a rhythm to all of his rituals that I don't even think he's aware of. I woke up today from his tapping. He was shaving: he clicks the razor on the sink twice, shaves for a bit, clicks the razor four times, two, four, two, four. He then brushes his teeth and taps his toothbrush two times. This all happens after his shower and a loud nose-blowing session. He then cleans his ears with two Q-tips that he folds in half and leaves on the sink. He even dries off the same way every morning: chest on down and then up the back. This is why it drives him crazy when I don't put things back in the same place. Last week I heard him grumbling in the shower that we didn't have any "fucking" soap ("Jesus, do I have to do everything around here?") when all along the soap was located in the opposite corner from its usual resting place. That he never, ever misplaces his keys is one of the perks of living with him. I lose my keys often.

When I was in the hospital, trying not to have Luke, I had a night nurse who was a lot like Sean. All of her equipment was in a neat belt around her waist and she always put me to sleep in the same manner each night. She made marks with ballpoint pen on my styrofoam cup to indicate how much I drank. She moved with precision and certainty. Everything was calm and matter-of-fact. Part of why I was able to stay in labor for over a week was because the rhythm of her ritual eased my mind. It's likely why Luke was born on a Saturday at nine a.m. That nurse had the Friday night before off. It's funny that I don't remember her name, but I remember that she had two little boys and that their names were Gregory and Timothy: Both three syllables, both ending in Y.

July 24

We spent the day at Wirth Park, swimming. Now we are all sunburned and thirsty. There aren't any groceries in the house, not even bottles of water. It's hard to believe that it has been a full year since Lizzie almost drowned at Wirth Park. She jumped off the high dive without knowing how to really swim. Today, neither one of us can think about that day without getting queasy. It was good then, to go today to have her realize that she could still have fun swimming (as long as she stays on the shallow end). The kids ate hotdogs and warm salty pretzels, and sat, wrapped in wet towels, their red chlorine filled eyes staring off towards the pool, not really focusing on anything in particular.

I did not eat hotdogs. I'm officially sick of food. This happens to me every summer. I just get to the point where nothing sounds good. It's even worse without the kitchen. The first time I remember feeling this way about food was one summer watching my dad play softball. My mom was there, as well as my aunt Shirley. We watched the game and tried, unsuccessfully, to name any food at all that might sound good. Once the kitchen is finished, I don't think I will ever eat another cheeseburger or slice of pizza ever again.

The only thing that sounds good really, is the kind of lemonade that I can get at festivals: where they squeeze two halves of a lemon into sugar water and then shake it like crazy between two clear glasses. Making it for myself doesn't taste right. There is no substitute for the official shakers. The only thing that ever came close was the purple grape juice I drank when I was pregnant with Elizabeth. I remember Christmas vacation, sitting on the couch, pouring glass after glass of freezing cold grape juice over crushed ice, sipping it with a straw, and feeling that all was right with the world. It is probably also why I gained forty pounds during that pregnancy.

I can eat two other things when nothing else sounds good. One is a baked potato with butter, sour cream, and salt. The other is corn on the cob, slightly burnt, also from a festival. Maybe when I am super rich, I will just hold a year round festival in my backyard, or as the super rich might say, "on the grounds." Meanwhile, I am fine drinking Blue Moon beer from semi-cold bottles, reading *Gourmet* magazine, and breathing a long, previously suppressed sigh, that no one even came close to drowning today.

July 25

Last night I saw the website of where we are staying in Costa Rica. It is gorgeous and I am excited, and mildly terrified. I noticed that our plan includes things like repelling down waterfalls, which are located in the rainforest (where snakes and monkeys and butterflies bigger than basketballs dwell).

I was soaking my still sunburned back in the tub when Sean walked in. I told him that I am going to need to be in really, really, great shape for the trip and he said that it is only five months away. I said I thought that was enough time and he said, "For what? To develop cat-like reflexes?"

It's true. I have a history of being a bit clumsy. Sean doesn't know how I plan to hike up a volcano when I can't normally grocery shop (or as he says, "step down a curb") without falling. I don't know either, but I know I will. Even though I might be clumsy and sore (and stagnant and hurting and easily winded), I am also determined. If I am in a setting where everyone else is gliding down a telephone wire in an Easter basket and it looks like fun, I will do it (unless it involves some sort of bungee jump; that's out).

So I am putting all of my focus and attention on feeling gazelle-like: a wispy, floating ballerina who can move like one of Charlie's angels. My cat-like reflexes will surprise everybody.

July 26

Today, I discovered why people like me, who enjoy rummage sales and surprises, Craigslist and bargains should not even start playing around on eBay. I am officially addicted. I am also super pissed off because someone outbid me for the vintage Lake George Crew Team hooded sweatshirt.

Bidding on eBay reminded me of that short story my dad once read to me (must have been Ray Bradbury, but not *Fahrenheit 451*) about computers taking over society. The main character had not even seen his own mother in years because all of their contact was via technology. I remember him reading it to me when I was very young and it seemed like such a crazy thought. Now it doesn't seem so far fetched. I am still waiting for the day when I can somehow pee via Bluetooth.

I also remembered hearing someone's comedy routine about how many of the things from the cartoon *The Jetsons* are now true. The comic got a big laugh when he interrupted his observations with, "Where is my flying car? I want my flying car, dammit!"

So many of the things that I wished for when Luke was a baby (groceries delivered to my door, drive through Starbucks, drive through post office) now exist. When he was born, we not did have Internet or email, not even a cell phone to text with. "When I was your age, I had to walk fourteen miles in the bitter cold to get to school..." Yeah, I guess it happens with each generation, milestones of bittersweet progress.

It's probably good that I didn't have Internet access when Luke was in that incubator. I would have driven myself nuts researching all of the terrible things that might happen to him. Instead, I was able to focus on him, just him, without any outside influence (except for a boring book from the hospital gift store about "What to Expect in the Neonatal Intensive Care Unit). On the flip side, I probably could have found him darling, unbelievably tiny clothes on eBay.

July 27

I often have dreams that take place in the same location: Six Flags Great America, Lolo's kitchen on 72nd Street, or (like two nights ago), the parking lot at Northridge. For some reason, this is where we were supposed to park for Cathy's wedding shower.

In the dream, Cathy was to remarry a toad of a man (Cathy's teeth were chipped too) and I was holding my fourth child, a girl, who was not at all cute. It looked like she had hair plugs and even though she had just been born she could say, "Hi, Dada." It was creepy. I was holding her at the shower and trying to feed her a bottle, but she wanted milk from a cup and then she started to eat everything: appliances, the flowers from a flowerpot. I started to panic and called for Cathy's sister-in-law, a pediatrician, who was in a back bedroom. She said, "Oh, yes, that baby has Munchausen's disease." The dream ended here.

Turns out, Munchausen's syndrome is a psychiatric disorder in which those affected feign disease or trauma in order to draw attention or sympathy. Why did I dream this? The answer has both eluded and haunted me for two days now. On so many levels too, starting with the hair plugs, but most definitely ending with the fact that somewhere in my subconscious I have given birth to a needy, attention grabbing, sick child.

Do most people dream this vividly, this specifically? Am I so oblivious in my waking hours that I need my subconscious to kick my ass? The weird part is that sometimes when I dream, I wake up, scared, startled. That happened last night too, but when I woke up, I felt some kind of heavy energy in our right bedroom corner. I was wide awake, but I could see a thin, pen-like blade

97

(almost like the clip on a pen) spinning back and forth and I had a sudden understanding that I should purchase pineapple juice because it would lead to ten thousand dollars. This is crazy, I understand. Still, things like this have forced me into really believing that there is no time and space, that we truly are multi-dimensional beings. They have also forced to me a big believer in Tylenol PM.

July 28

My aunt and uncle brought over some cool Batman pajamas for William, as a birthday present. It was odd that he didn't go nuts over them because he loves presents and always says thank you. In fact, it's kind of funny because he says, "Thank you, Grandma, Thank you, Grandpa, Thank you (fill in the blank) after every single gift. I saw him look at the pajamas and make kind of a concerned face. He only thanked John and Shirley after I reminded him too.

Later that night when it was time to get ready for bed, I asked him which of the two new Batman patterns he wanted to wear first. He hesitated before telling me, "Those pajamas start on fire. Why do they want me to be on fire?" I had no idea what he meant until I saw the bright yellow tag on the side of the pajamas that said "FIRE RESISTANT" in big black letters. I explained what resistant meant and now he is very excited about his pajamas.

I had a similar experience at a restaurant last week when I ordered a drink that spelled, "betelegeuse," which I took to be a pun on the name Bella Lugosi, which is how I pronounced my order: betel-LOO-GAY-Z. It turns out that betelegeuse is just Beetle Juice. Dumb. The waitress probably didn't even know who Bella Lugosi was and more than likely believed me to have a speech impediment.

Things like that have happened to me often in life, like when I was three and Lolo asked me how my aunt Mary was feeling and I told her that she had a Kleenex stuck in her. I guess that what really happened was that she had some soft tissue removed.

Everyone laughed about that for many years. I remember feeling stupid that everyone laughed, so I have tried not to laugh too hard at William thinking that he'd burst into flames wearing those pajamas. I did take a picture, however: William, arms spread wide open, grinning ear to ear, proudly displaying the black bat on his chest, more grateful than ever to be flame resistant.

July 29

Sean talked for a long while tonight to a friend from back home. He laughed and laughed guffaws that shook the house and made Luke and I giggle. When this friend came to our wedding in 1997, his wife went dress shopping and got caught in the rain. It rained and stormed (it even flooded) the entire weekend they were in town. Everyone told us that rain meant good luck; guess we needed buckets of it.

Each time he calls Sean, it marks time for me too somehow, as even I have known him for almost twenty years. Since our wedding, he has married twice, divorced twice, started a business, left a business, had two children, become a security guard, bought a gun, and now dates a "dancer," ten years his junior. I guess our lives are a bit ordinary in comparison.

I wonder if when Sean talks to him, if there is a distant piece of his mind wishing that he were dating a twenty-seven year old dancer. I wonder if he feels caged in, crabby that I hate guns, bored with the routine of our lives, bored that I love routine, embarrassed to ever be driving my SUV that is plastered with an OBAMA '08 bumper sticker. I know he loves us; I know ninety-nine percent of him wouldn't trade places with anyone, but there must be a one percent that aches for a wild freedom that I don't understand or hope for.

Really, when I think about it, I can look at anyone else's life and rewind it a decade or so, and no matter who it is, I am in awe of how much happens in such a short time. Babies, jobs, connections, moves, divorces, marriages, scandals, deaths, wounds, elation, diseases, adventures, hook ups, break ups. It astounds me that in a year, both of my parents will be sixty. That is about how old Lolo was when we took our first road trip out west.

I spend a great deal of time wanting things to hurry up. I want the dream. Dream house, dream car, dream job, dream body, dream dogs, dream money, dream cleaning lady, dream personal chef, dream person to dry my hair each morning. I do want these things NOW, the sooner, the better. I wonder if there is a way to get them and make time stand still simultaneously.

There will come a time, I imagine, when I will be telling my own children that rain on their wedding day is good luck. Will I have spent the time between then and now wishing and wanting instead of doing or am I "doing" already and just not paying attention?

Right before that road trip out west, more than thirty years ago, I sat with my dad and Christopher at our kitchen table in the house on Forty-Ninth Street. Together, we made up a game: a long list of crazy, specific things we should look for over the course of the drive. We listed things like, "very fat woman pushing a grocery cart," or "black and white dog walking with a man in a brown vest." Whoever spotted these things on our trip would earn one point per sighting. The winner would be the person with the most points. We all loaded up into Lolo's 1972 olive green Oldsmobile, no air conditioning, no seatbelts, cream soda and Brach caramels in a cooler in the back. I sat with a Steno notebook in my lap and began journaling the trip (I recorded what each person ordered at each restaurant for over two weeks). In between writing and playing Old Maid with Lolo, I'd keep one eye open to find something on the list. Everyone played, all five of us. It was very competitive.

I remember some of the details from our various destinations, but not the details one is really supposed to remember. I remember playing with a puddle jumper in a backyard in Sun Valley, Idaho, learning to play Uno, discovering I could tie a cherry stem with my tongue. I remember how hot the car was, getting my hair knotted up in a headband, the smell of sulfur at Yellowstone, the moose that walked in front of our car. I remember looking through the AAA book to find hotels that had at least three stars and listed a pool. I can remember each hotel room that we stayed in. I remember misspelling stomachache in my journal ("stomache") and everyone laughing at that. I remember riding in the car going to buy Tums.

I only remember one thing about the ride home. I remember that we were sick of eating out. We found a restaurant that served homemade soup, which we all ordered, and ate in silence and gratitude.

We could have gone anywhere on that vacation. What made the time in the car more memorable than the landmarks we visited was that we approached it with the intention that it was going to be an adventure, a fun game. That trip is my purest reminder that it's not the destination, nor is it the journey. It is in the creation. That is where dreams form and desire engages. It begins with a list, or a flood, or a bowl of pea soup, or with the whisper of a belief that rain means good luck.

July 30

William and I got the giggles today at the pediatrician's office. He had to leave a urine sample. He had to pee so badly, but the idea of peeing in a cup was so funny to him that he had to hold his crotch with both hands to keep himself from wetting his pants. Each time he gained his composure to try to take his pants off, he'd start to giggle, and we'd start all over again. Eventually, he was able to squeak his pants down just a crack below firing point and he peed straight forward towards the back of the toilet seat. I tried my best to hold the plastic cup horizontally. It was like trying to stop an overflowing fire hydrant with a thimble. We were both laughing so hard and I was swearing. I did my best to clean up the mess and then I washed my hands about forty times. The nurse was waiting for us when we opened the door.

The rest of the visit was uneventful, except for the part where I defended myself for not still using a booster seat and the part where the doctor had to look in Will's underwear. He was anticipating this, I know, because he actually *wore* underwear (he frequently forgets to), and because when the doctor finally did it, Will gave me a sly, lopsided grin and raised his eyebrows. On our car ride to the appointment, he asked me why the doctor has to look into his underwear and I didn't really have an answer for him. I mean, honestly, do doctors really, ever take that millisecond peek and then say with shock and horror, "OH MY GOD! WHAT IS GOING ON DOWN THERE?"

Luke's annual appointment is tomorrow and he is worried about a "girl doctor" looking inside his underwear, especially because last year he wasn't exactly able to control the "mood," let's say, of his "parts." We spent our twenty minutes in the small patient room having him jump up and down and think about things like football and car crashes to try to have his anatomy obey his mind. There was a mother and son moment I wouldn't mind forgetting.

So after tomorrow, all doctor and dentist appointments are caught up, the end of yet another cycle. As William and I waited today, we heard tiny babies screaming from their immunizations and I flashed back to the first pediatrician visit I made with three kids, a double stroller, leaking breasts, and about five different purses and diaper bags. I barely made it down the corridor of numbered doors without crying. Catching flying pee mid-air and praying for underwear to deflate is nothing in comparison with that.

July 31

We went to Lolo's tonight for dinner. She worries that we don't have a kitchen, so at ninety-one years old, she cooks a giant meal in her apartment a few times a month, calls me and tells me to be over at six. About ten minutes into the meal, William excused himself and went to the bathroom where he proceeded to clog up the toilet.

Lolo and I went in there and used the plunger, but no matter how hard we tried, we could not get his giant turd to make its way down her pipes. I wondered aloud how large could a seven year old's poop actually be, and Lolo giggled. She turned out to be a much more aggressive plunger than I was. Her arms, I discovered, are incredibly strong. She plunged with the vigor of a twenty-year-old frat boy.

Yesterday my mom took her to her doctor and he told them that my grandma would need to start giving herself insulin shots, as her diabetes is now beyond the point of controlling by diet alone. The doctor was a real ass because when my mom asked what to do if Lolo was not able to give herself injections, he just shrugged and said, "Institutionalize her." We heard this after his nurse told my grandma that she did not even have an appointment that day and then turned to my mom and said, "You know how *they* can forget."

I do not understand why people treat old people as if they haven't lived. My grandmother grew up without a mother, a crappy father; she ran away with her sister to Chicago and lived, basically, on the streets. She got married at sixteen, had her first baby at seventeen. She survived the Depression, losing her husband to cancer, two bouts of breast cancer, the loss of a two-year-old grandchild to adoption, a heart attack. She delivered my aunt at home, on a bed of newspapers, with only her sister there to help. She has lived long enough to watch most of her friends, and even a daughter-in-law, die. This woman worked full time until she was in her eighties, and only recently gave up her car and gave in to having a woman come to clean her apartment once a week. She has lived and loved and continues to do so, fully.

So, even if she did forget to call to reschedule an appointment (which she didn't), she does not need to be treated like a child whose parent has the need to spell out C-A-N-D-Y instead of saying the word. The truth is her diabetes has caught up to her and she needs to be more aggressive in dealing with it. That doctor might have said, "There are some serious side effects by not using insulin. I realize that no one really looks forward to giving themselves injections, but this is a manageable disease and I would be glad to send over someone to teach you more about insulin and how to self treat." Instead, he treated her as if she could not understand English and chose to address my mother instead.

Our State Fair is famous for its cream puffs. It is the one thing that my Grandma always craves this time of year. She is too old to really enjoy going to the fair these days, but she sees the cream puffs on T.V. and longs for one. Our local baker makes delicious ones this week to celebrate the Fair and last year I surprised Lolo with one. On our way to her house, I called her and said, "So, I suppose with this diabetes news, you probably don't want me to bring you a cream puff." She immediately said, "No. I could really use a cream puff." The joy, I suppose of living for over ninety years is knowing, really knowing, when to tell your doctor to fuck off.

107

August 1

When we were driving to Lolo's last night, William did not feel well. His ear was really bothering him, to the point where he would punch himself in the ear and yell, "Why me? Why is it always me!" We were stuck in terrible traffic and Will was getting super ornery. He kept shifting positions and screaming, "IT HURTS!" He started a long monologue addressed to God. *"Why do you do this to me, GOD? Why me? Well, you know what, God? F.U!!!!! F.U."* I didn't even know what to say to that. He was upset beyond anything I could comfort or reprimand.

By the time we finally arrived at my Grandma's, he had calmed down. Thankfully, too, as about nine other residents were sitting outside the building. They kept getting Elizabeth to try to drop the cake box with the creampuffs in it. One gentleman told me five separate times, "Do you know they want $3.50 for one of those at the fair. $3.50!" This didn't really strike me as an unreasonable amount, so I tried to imagine being ninety (forty-two years from now) and what creampuff price tag would shock me. I settled on sixteen dollars. If creampuffs are ever sixteen dollars, I will ban them.

If that man had sticker shock over a pastry, I can imagine the face he might make if he overheard William telling God to stick it. Back in the day, I suppose, there was no such thing as Sensory Integration Disorder. I wonder how the world might change even more by the time I really am ninety. Maybe, be then, Dairy Queen, will allow their employees to sprinkle M&M's on vanilla ice cream cones.

It must be my week to have conversations with elderly men. Today, while William and I were eating breakfast at the bagel store, a man sat across from us. He wanted to know why we were up so early in the summer. "School hasn't started yet, has it?" he puzzled. I explained that William attends a four-week summer morning program. He thought this was good and then said to William, "I'll tell you a secret. When you are older, find out what books your teacher is going to have you read during the year and then read 'em in the summer. That way, you won't have so much homework." He tapped his temple and William just stared at him.

William's ear was fine today. I don't know why it bothered him for such a short spell. Maybe he got God's attention.

August 2

When twelve or thirteen, maybe older, I ran five miles in the Al Maguire Run. I trained with my parents, up Concordia to Roosevelt, around the boulevard and back. At the end of each run, I would lie in the front yard and feel my entire body pulse. This was the only part about running that I liked, the end, because that's when my whole body felt alive. Hearing my heart beat between my ears always reminded me of big drums in the Christmas parade.

I used to take walks with my dad. Once, in the middle of winter, we walked to a playground and spelled out our names with our footsteps in the snow. "Kelly and Greg" filled the playground and when we were done, I went on the slide, in the dead calm of winter night sky, and I flew off its icy surface.

Even when Luke started kindergarten, I'd walk him to school. In the last few years, walking has become laborious. I don't know if it happened after my foot surgery or not, but I cannot seem to walk quickly or without acute attention to the physical pains I feel. Today we walked for about a mile. My thighs rubbed together like two fat sticks anxious for fire. I couldn't even make it four blocks without intense, all consuming, sluggishness. It's almost like trying to walk through thick mud. Instead of looking forward to our trip next week, I look for comfortable walking shoes and worry about the heat.

I am at a loss for how to address this issue. I have spent hours at gyms, with trainers. I have done pilates and yoga, soul clearings, reiki, flower essence therapy, sugar free diets, naturopathy, acupuncture. I just want to be able to really move, to run. The last time I tried to run outdoors, a gerbil could have beat me to the corner. I felt like Eddie Murphy's character, Sherman, from *The Nutty Professor.* For some reason, I can run for thirty minutes on an elliptical machine, but get me outside, and I'm Jello. I noticed it a lot when I was in Maryland last April, trying to keep up with a bunch of other teachers, most of them fifteen years older than me.

When I was with Marcos, a former student, in New York a few years ago now, a friend of his mom's walked behind me. She was an acupuncturist. She yelled at me about my shoes and made me wear her hiking boots. She also told me to walk through the pain and it would go away. Perhaps that is what I do: tiptoe around the pain, expecting it, avoiding it. The solution might be in facing it head on, walking every day.

I would like to feel again, the way I felt flying off that winter slide. It was one of the few times in my entire life I felt weightless.

August 3

We dropped Luke off at camp today. He will be gone for two weeks. He has a great cabin, right on the lake, and as a plus this year, a private bathroom. Even I would camp if there were plumbing. Sean turned our backyard into a campground for the other kids, so that they, too, would have a taste of the outdoors. He put up tiki torches and a tent, a circle of chairs, and a mini bonfire. At first, I felt guilty, as if we really should take the kids camping. But after two s'mores and about forty mosquito bites, I changed my mind. Even Lizzie and Will only made it in the tent for an hour or so until they complained of back pain.

It is probably good practice for me to start leaving Luke for chunks at a time, forcing me to realize that he has his own life, that my life is separate from his. That is so difficult to do. I want so much to have some kind of spy camera to see what he is doing every moment. What is he doing now? Is he having trouble sleeping his first night? What is he thinking about? Is he scared at all, even a little bit? Did I pack warm enough pajamas?

He wanted to spend his "last night" at Grandma and Grandpa's. He and my dad watched *Harold and Kumar 2*, which I find hilarious, especially because my dad has strong opposition to Luke seeing *Dark Knight*, the latest Batman movie. Regardless, they watched the movie, looked at the stars at one in the morning, took a five-mile bike ride, made homemade doughnuts. I cannot blame him for wanting his last taste of the "real world" to be at their house.

I remember feeling that way about Grandma Lois. Whenever we would drive from Missouri to Milwaukee, I would sleep in her bed, wear her nightgowns, stare at the picture of crucified Jesus, and talk and talk until Lolo finally started snoring. I had a student last year that created a drawing of a little boy holding a sign that read, "Hooray for Grandparents."

My kids are so lucky. They are the only grandchildren on both sides of the family. They have two grandpas, three grandmas, and one great grandma. They are even old enough to remember their Great Grandma Jean. All of these ties to love have created the loveliest of childhood memories for the kids: pie making, jet skiing, boat rides, lawn mower rides, packages arriving on the front porch, video gaming stations received for birthdays, cakes made with love. Hooray for grandparents, indeed.

August 4

There were very loud thunderstorms last night. I kept waking up and I worried about whether or not the strength of the storm was scaring Luke, far away, for his first night in a camp cabin with strangers. I wondered what he was thinking about, or if he was even awake. I wondered if any part of him felt at all homesick or was curious about what we were doing.

Around two in the morning, furious thunder startled me and I realized that William's little 1950's armchair was still in the backyard. I swore, audibly, and Sean asked what was the matter. I told him, but he just said, "So fucking what."

I also noted the official start of my mom's birthday and remembered another birthday of hers when it was storming and we ate at a super fancy restaurant downtown. The dining room had all glass, floor-to-ceiling windows, and as we ate, rain pounded against the glass, and the weather lit up the entire sky like little birthday bombs.

Having a son old enough to be on his own, not needing to be tucked in or kissed goodnight, and a lonely, wet, Archie Bunker chair, bought with love and affection at an early morning rummage sale, soaking in a summer storm, plus thoughts of a birthday dinner from twenty years earlier all made me feel old and heavy. The rain, partly, was to blame for the crushing feelings of nostalgia and loss.

Even though my energy has been low all week, the storm also reminded me that rain is lucky. I hoped that Luke remembered that I said that once, so that as he lay there, in a small cabin in the dark with five other boys that he just met, that he would feel adventurous and lucky, not frightened in the least, not even giving me a thought at all. I know there are mothers out there who have to worry about sons away at war, or in jail for a crime they might not have committed, and that my worries are small in comparison; it is sleep-away camp, after all. I don't know why it feels like my job to worry, as if I would be neglectful if I didn't. Worry is an odd sensation because it doesn't really serve any purpose other than to make the worrier ill at ease.

Knowing this makes it easier to hope. The only way I could fall back asleep was by imagining Luke cracking jokes with his new found friends, not a bully among them, farting under covers, telling crude jokes, and ultimately falling asleep to the steady lullaby of raindrops, and as lightning would light up the sky, Luke would think to himself, "Happy Birthday, Grandma."

August 5

Elizabeth donated twelve inches and three pounds of her hair today. Sarah cut the waist length ponytail at the nape of Elizabeth's neck. It was very exciting and Elizabeth loved it. I asked her how she felt and she replied, "Free."

Later, we all went to dinner with Lolo, my folks, and Michael and Lori, my aunt and uncle, who were in from Colorado. The two kids were patient with the long, fancy dinner. Elizabeth excused herself about five different times to go to the bathroom to look in the mirror.

On the way home, she and William shared my iPod. They listened to the song *Closer to Me*, by Dar Williams. They lyrics are "What can you do with a day? What will you wake up and see?"

Elizabeth thought she was singing, "Will you wake up fancy?" She said, "I love that part where she wakes up fancy." I imagine that is how her new hair makes her feel.

The irony, for me, is that the next line of that song is "The farther you get, the closer to me." So it goes. The freer Elizabeth feels, the more space she takes up in my heart. August 5th: Elizabeth can put her own ponytail in. Independence has never been so bittersweet.

August 6

Earlier today, Lolo was sitting out on her patio with Lori and Michael. "Lori," she said, "water these flowers," which Lori dutifully did. Lolo pointed to a pot in the corner, "Those only need a little bit of water. They have been growing so nicely." Lori walked over to the pot, 'But, Mom," she said, "These are silk flowers." Lolo insisted that they were real. She told Lori that these flowers were very tiny when she first got them. Lori put the pot of fake flowers on my grandma's lap and had her touch them. My grandma stared and stared at them, in complete disbelief. She wondered aloud if perhaps a bird had dropped seeds into the pot at one time. Lori asked, "What, a bird with Pansy seeds?" She and Michael could not help but laugh.

Later tonight, while we were all over at Lolo's, Lori told this story and we all laughed big belly laughs. We told Grandma that she wouldn't be able to live this story down.

Lolo, still partially convinced that those pansies were real, sipped large spoonfuls of Cherry Bounce (Door County cherries soaked and aged in a jug of vodka) as a part of her wondered, I'm sure, if she had officially begun to lose her marbles.

August 7

Sean just came back from the mall. He had wanted to buy some prescription sunglasses before we head out to Vegas. He said he was the only customer in the place and there were five salespersons. One of them asked Sean if he needed some help and Sean said, "Well, I need to get some sunglasses." The salesman replied, "What do you use them for?" At that point, Sean left the store. I can imagine what he was thinking: "Why, I use them as bookends of course," or something along those lines.

I haven't really done anything to get ready for our trip, except that I got a pedicure. I did clean the house today because I hate going away and coming home to a dirty house. I don't want to go away, feel all happy and relaxed and come home to a shit hole. It's bad enough that there won't be a kitchen.

I did manage to slice a good chunk of my finger off while cleaning. I slammed it in the kids' bedroom door. I won't clean that one room anymore because no matter how many times I've tried to make it organized and cute, those two tear it apart. No one can walk in there without stepping on something, usually a bottle cap or something with wheels. Therefore, I slammed the door (out of sight, out of mind), catching my finger in the latch. I guess it's good that I didn't get a manicure too, as the nail on my index finger no longer exists.

I couldn't find any Band-Aids. The only thing in the First Aid kit was a tube of toothpaste. I kept bleeding all over the floor I had just cleaned, all over the freshly folded washcloths. Finally, I found a smiley face yellow bandage that William saved in the back of the vanity. It barely covered the wound. All I could hear in my head is what Sean would have said about my lack of preparedness. I swear to God that his shop must have four fully stocked first aid kits. Last week, his friend got his arm caught in the router machine, and the guys knew just what to do while they waited for the ambulance. Later, I told Elizabeth that somebody knew to hold the artery under the arm to control the bleeding. She asked me what an artery was and I discovered that I really have no idea.

Even though Sean wasn't home during the finger accident, he might as well have been because William was here, who is basically Sean's "Mini Me." He, at least, knew where the two first aid kits were, albeit empty ones. He told me not to worry, that he would help me. "I feel sorry for you, Mom," as he ran cold water for me, while Lizzie made gagging noises from the hallway. He looked at the wound and told me that I wouldn't need stitches. He even found some gauze to stop the bleeding.

Though Will has his fair share of struggle, personal demons even, it's nice to know that he will never be the type of person who asks anyone else what they use sunglasses for.

August 8

My mom's show opened tonight. This series of paintings, wide open and abstract, are linked to her rabbit drawings. It's fun to walk from painting to painting, finding a bunny foot or tail here or there. One of my favorites shows just the tracks, traces of the rabbit's presence. She ended her artist statement by saying that for her, the rabbits are a way back to enchantment.

The rabbits, for me, link me to the mother that I have always had. The rabbits, for me, mean family. When I look at these paintings, I see my mom, thirty-five years ago, weaving found trinkets into macramé on her bedroom wall. I see her working in her garage on the potter's wheel. I see her sewing ducks onto checkerboard watercolor paper at the dining room table, or collecting wildflowers for still lives as we walked along Scuppernong Trail.

Art has surrounded me since I was born: a mustached, ceramic planter, pink flamingo sculptures (I hated those), an oil painting of circles, all in seventies colors, a yellow, orange, and blue geometric painting that hung in our kitchen on Forty-Ninth street. (Friends would come over and try to guess what it was.) The rabbits in her latest work make me think of the artist that has waited inside my mother, waited to come out until she had room to breathe on her own. They are playful and raw; they play peek-a-boo, and occasionally even tell a tragic tale or two (or at least they do for me and my love of narration).

They also remind me of Lolo's bathroom. She has (and has for decades now; I remember the remodel) framed pictures of rabbits hanging on the bathroom wall. There was a huge mirror in there, and a hand mirror (that she still has) that shows the way you really are on one side, and a magnified self on the other. She had great makeup in the first drawer of the vanity, and always a great big fluffy rug on the floor. Every time I peed in that bathroom, I'd stare at the bunnies on the wall.

Even though my mom's work isn't about my grandma's bathroom, her rabbits always make me feel like I am part of an amazing generation of women. Elizabeth didn't have money to buy my mom flowers for the opening, so instead, she made some out of plastic knives and paper plates. As I watched her solve this dilemma ("I have to bring her flowers. How can I do it?), I saw the artist in her and was glad to know that she is one of us, too.

She and William helped me skewer fresh mozzarella, basil, and tomatoes to put on platters to bring to the reception. As I piled up the food, William stopped and said, "It is really looking so beautiful." I love that my kids have eyes for these sorts of things, that they pay attention to beauty. William's favorite painting tonight was one that almost looked like a bird in flight. I can understand why he likes that work so much; he feels himself there.

It was amazing to take part in the evening, to see so many of my mom's friends and family there to celebrate her work. I love watching the red "sold" dots appear out of nowhere underneath certain works, sparking my curiosity (Who bought that? Where will it hang?). After Susie's mom read my mom's statement, she cried and even bought a painting.

On the drive to the gallery, I reminded Elizabeth and William that the night might end up feeling long, but that they were expected to be their best selves because it was a very important night to their grandma. William asked if it was okay to laugh there and I assured him that it was. "Loud?" he asked. I told him he could laugh as loudly as he wanted to, as long as it was genuine. Elizabeth asked if grandma would be giving a speech about the work and I told her that no, tonight was just for looking. She asked if it would be dark or if the lights would be on. I realized that she thought "show," might indicate "movie." I told her that the lights would be on, like at the art museum. She turned to William and said, "We can't run around or scream. That would be very rude," she paused and then added, "Because tonight is Grandma's moment."

That it was.

August 9

We leave for Las Vegas in the morning. Elizabeth, Will, and even Greta will stay with my mom and dad. The kids are excited, but apprehensive about us leaving, as well. Elizabeth stuck a drawing of herself crying big black Sharpie tears inside of my suitcase. On it, she scrawled, "Bees knees, cats pajamas," which is how we always say goodnight to each other.

I went to another Mary meeting this morning. I asked Mary why I am so out of my body, why walking sometimes feels like sinking. The answer was long, but basically translated to the fact that I don't live inside my body, too uncomfortable. They also indicated that there were so many layers to this issue, we will need to work together privately. I translated that to mean, "You are so fucked up that you need a private session." My brother translated it to mean that the information they wanted to share was private and they did not want to embarrass me in front of the group. I don't know. I've given birth in front of a the entire neonatal staff at St. Joe's hospital; I don't think there is much after that that will embarrass me in front of strangers.

After Mary, I had a headache and felt nauseous. I felt both overwhelmed and ambivalent about packing and all that there was still to do to prepare for the trip. I literally just checked out and slept on the couch. Afterwards, instead of packing or doing the bills or the laundry or anything else pressing, I downloaded season six of *Curb Your Enthusiasm* to my iPod. Sometimes after a day of being told that there isn't any easy answer, a day where I spent twenty five minutes in a fitting room next to two girls who were the female version of *Beavis and Butthead*, a day where nothing just fell into place, I needed a little Larry David.

Larry David and a note from Elizabeth that let me know that someone out there thinks I am the bee's knees.

August 14

We are back. I purposely decided not to write while we were away; I feared it might turn into a big, blubbery diary of what we ate and saw. I thought it might be wiser to sum up the trip at the very end. Now, I am regretting that decision a bit, as it feels like we have been gone for weeks, not days, and writing feels unfamiliar to me. To dive back in, however, I have decided to make a list of the things I know about myself now that I didn't on August 9th (my last entry):

- I am a better lounger than a sightseer.

- We have a fantastic bed that nothing in the world, not even a five star hotel with a four thousand dollar duvet on a king sized-pillow topped one can even come close to in excellence or comfort. In fact, at the second night of our stay, Sean woke up and exclaimed, "This bed is HUGE."

- I like who I am. Many people irritate me.

- I HATE waiting (I knew this already) and LINES (knew that too) and being called Mrs. Mizer (didn't know that until now).

- I like toffee pudding.

- If I lived near slot machines, I'd have an addiction problem.

- I hate Las Vegas.

- I do not particularly enjoy heights. Sean and I took a twenty-four dollar elevator ride to the top of Fake Eiffel Tower and I got sick and panicky. We barely got out of the elevator.

- Corona really is the best beer for one hundred and ten degree weather.

- The human body is capable of extraordinary, animalistic possibilities. If a person performing *Le Reve* can dive thousands of feet from invisible heights into a swimming pool that only moments before was a solid stage, I should be able to walk on my foot. Amazing.

- I love good hotel bathrooms. I hate public bathroom soap and especially am irritated by automated soap dispensers that are intended to work with a wave of the palm, but do not and I end up looking like a fool, waving to a bathroom fixture.

- Sean is really losing his hearing, left ear to be specific.

- *"Curb Your Enthusiasm"* is officially the best way to kill time on a plane and is very fun to watch if you share earplugs and take turns holding the iPod. Sean and I laughed until the plane shook, I think, especially at the episode where Larry David tells the gastroenterologist that he stuck a gerbil up his ass.

- Prolonged exposure to cigar smoke makes me nauseous.

- I like a lamp next to my side of the bed.

126

- When we move, I want a bathroom with two sinks and a makeup mirror.

Lastly, I love, really love, from the deepest part of my insides, living in Milwaukee. I can get off the plane and my luggage is ready immediately. I catch a cab without waiting or whistles or valets. People are friendly and funny. No one here is stuck working in a tourist trap and I can buy an entire case of Corona for six dollars. I like it most of all because it is home and walking back into it feels like falling into fresh white snow to make snow angels for the first time.

We saw some friends today who had just returned from Sri Lanka, where they spent the summer with relatives. Their middle son, Luke's friend, had a very difficult time coming back to the states. He cried at the airport. Even though he is coming back to school and friends, he left his grandma and aunts behind. It will be two years before he sees them again. That is a very long time to wait for a piece of one's heart to fall back into place, hovering just above a memory. For him, returning to Milwaukee airport didn't feel the same as making snow angels at all. It must have felt like he was being sent to the principal's office.

August 15

Today a boy was nearly killed by a car, right in front of me. The car stopped within an inch of his bike.

Later, Michael Phelps won his seventh Olympic gold medal by 1/100 of a second, the length of a fingernail, and I watched a driver ignore flashing red railroad lights as he zoomed across the bumpy train tracks, a train barely missing him.

I wondered if so much was possible in the blink of a moment, if the way I think about things (even the smallest of things: zit cream, mold on washcloths, fog, raspberries losing their flavor) if it changes the outcome. Are fate and freewill even more closely intertwined than I previously imagined?

August 16

We watched the Olympics again tonight, mostly the women's marathon race. Elizabeth noted that the T.V. screen read "Live."

"Live?" she asked, "This is happening *right* now?" I told her that it was indeed.

"But it's light out!" she protested.

"Yes," I agreed, "it was light out."

She turned her head away from the screen and looked at me with complete disbelief, "The Chinese are nocturnal?"

I heard Sean laugh from upstairs and I tried not to laugh, as not to embarrass her and did my best to explain that in China, it's morning when it is night time in America.

Every so often, I'd get up out of the chair to do something (switch laundry, pour a drink of Gatorade) and I'd glance over at the couch. Sean and the boys took over the cushions and Lizzie lay draped over the narrow back edge. It is the first time we have had Luke home in fourteen days. Seeing everyone back at home and in the nest felt cozy and real: all little puzzle pieces back in the box. It was quiet, except for the hurried voice of the NBC sports announcer. I think all of us felt relief, just to have quiet togetherness, after days of chatter.

In Las Vegas, many tourists were taking photos and videos. We hardly took any, except for an occasional snapshot with Sean's iPhone. I don't understand excessive vacation pictures. The thing I want to remember most about the last week is not themed hotels or what my fancy bed looked like. I want to remember what is familiar now, but will be lost months from now, like the way Luke's hands looked to me when we picked him up from camp: bigger and tanner, marker scrawled over the top of one, faded red, knotted headband tied to the other wrist. The way Lizzie's body fit so perfectly across the narrow ledge of the sofa back, as if she were on a fancy poolside lounge chair, Sean's sunburned ears, now peeling, Greta asleep in a homemade space between William's armpit and the couch cushion, Lizzie's sweet voice asking innocent questions about the world at large. These things, I need to record.

Once, on our vacation, Sean and I went out for an expensive, fancy dinner. I recalled seeing a page from a magazine that I noticed years ago, which showcased a shelf in someone's house, where tiny, glass bottles containing sand lined a maple shelf. The labels on the outside of the bottles noted the locations that the homeowners had visited. "Cape Cod, 1989" was scrawled in delicate pen on one of them. I told Sean that I was going to save the cork from our wine bottle that evening as the first in a series of our own. We joked that we drank so much wine that the labels would be funny: "Tuesday, after work, Wednesday Lunch," and so on. I promised only to keep corks from special places, however, so now the one from Vegas sits at the bottom of my purse.

I wish it were just as simple to store and recall the other stuff. Videos, photographs, recordings (even saved wine corks) don't totally do it for me because, really, what I want to save are the things that touch our other senses: the way Will's furry back feels on my fingertips, the smell of chlorine in Lizzie's hair, or the tone of her voice as she asks me when we are going to see "Oldie-Locks," (my dad) next. I want to remember the way my heart stood still when I saw Luke again after two weeks and how it began to beat only upon hugging him. If I could bottle hearts, I'd be a billionaire. The closest I think I can get is to type on these pages. The nightly ritual of clicking on "File" and scrolling to "New Document" has become more than chronicled moments. It has become my prayer.

August 17

Sean and I were invited to a Lawn Bowling party next Friday night. On the phone, it sounded very Great Gatsby-like, and I envisioned us all sipping fancy, cool drinks, ice-cold water droplets sliding down thin glasses. That is until I heard that we needed to wear all white, as such garb is tradition. As someone who feels more comfortable dressing like Wednesday Addams than I do Daisy Buchanan, I was less than thrilled.

I'm sure that some people look fantastic in all white attire. Halle Berry, Beyonce, Jessica Lange, Posh Spice, for example, all don their size two whites with the glory of a race horse. Others should probably stay away from a monotonous absence of color: Edith Bunker and Jay Leno are two that come directly to my mind.

Today (because lawn bowling really does sound like fun), I tried on some white things and was able to come up with a list of about forty new ways to resemble a whale. I tried on one Isaac Mizrahi dress at Target and found that I bore a close resemblance to Nurse Ratched. I also tried on white pants of varying lengths. "ICE CREAM, ICE CREAM, ICE COLD ICE CREAM HERE!" I was tempted to shout as I inspected myself in the three-way mirror.

No, white is not for me. I'm not quite sure what I will do. Part of me is tempted to show up wearing "whatever," and then plead ignorance. "All white, you say? I am so sorry. I thought you said. Wear something "tight." Not that tight would be any better than white, really. Maybe I could suggest "Opposite Day," (a favorite *Sponge Bob Square Pants* episode of mine) and everyone could wear black: to hell with tradition! Doesn't grass stain white anyway? Aren't we on the LAWN? Maybe we should all wear green and play in a camouflaged league.

There's nothing like an end of the summer party to bring up all of my body image issues. When we were in Vegas, a woman kept trying to get me to buy one of those dresses that turns into a swim wrap that turns into a skirt that turns into a shirt things. I did not want to try it on and she couldn't understand why not. I told her that I would not look good in one of those things, but she insisted that yes, of course I would. I told her NO, that she looked good in one because she was very, very tiny and that anyone larger than her would look like wrapped cheese. She yanked the dress over my head to prove her point and then tied the empire waist high ribbons under my breasts. There I stood, in the full Las Vegas sun, looking like I was nine months pregnant, wrapped in some sort of sari. "See?" I said. She mumbled that I could untie the ribbons and just wear the shirt loose.

Too bad they didn't sell one in white. Had I known about this weekend, I would be all set.

August 18

It's was Greta's birthday today. I forgot until just this moment when I typed the date. She is five. We picked her out at a breeder at the end of October, when the kids were all so tiny. Luke was younger than Lizzie is now; that is hard to imagine even. The man who owned the place let all the puppies loose in the field and the kids were able to run with them. It was Sean, ultimately, who picked Greta from the pack.

We tried, that first night, to keep her crated, but Sean couldn't take the puppy cries. To this day, she sleeps in our bed, nestled between the cups of our knees, underneath all of the blankets. Three months after we got her, she ran between my feet as I was walking down the stairs with William, just two, on my hip. I tripped over her and the baby flew from my arms. I dove to save him, my hand behind his head. It was heroic to be sure, but I broke the top of my foot, which still swells to the size of a honeydew melon this time of year.

A broken foot, surgery on it a full year later, two toddlers, a puppy, a seven year old struggling to read ... it did not make for an easy few years. In retrospect, it wasn't the best time in our lives for a dog, but I had wanted the kids to grow up with one, not to know what it was even like to live without one. Goal completed. "Careful what you wish for," understood.

Just now, William woke up (it's just about midnight) screaming from pain in his ear. I think I have made the connection to his earaches with times that he listens to Luke's iPod. It must be too loud for such little ears. I tried to get William to swallow an ibuprophen gel cap, as I am out of any liquid stuff. He couldn't do it, which frustrated him and he cried harder and louder. Ultimately, I found an Alka Seltzer, which I split in half and had him drink. He thought that was fun and tasty. It also made him burp, which seemed to help his ear a little too. I tried to tuck him in bed, but he has at least one hundred stuffed animals on it. That must feel awful, like sleeping on uneven campground. I pushed half of them to the floor and did my best to make him cozy. I noticed that there was a half eaten pear on his floor and I repressed any desire to flip out about it. I leaned to kiss William's head and realized how small he really is: just a baby, really. He seems like such an old man sometimes, I can forget that he is only just seven.

Helping him with the earache (he continues to cry, get up, complain, lay back down, cry some more) exhausted me. I have no idea how I survived a time in our lives when both babies were up all the time and I had to let out a peeing puppy, limping the whole while. Sean and I joke that if we ever had a fourth baby we would name him Oblivious Cliff ("cousin to Curious George," Sean says) because he would have been conceived unintentionally, obliviously, and Cliff, for the one we'd both walk off of.

August 19

I finally ventured into Elizabeth and William's room today. The rotting pear ultimately made me understand I could no longer just shut the door to their happy chaos. I purchased one of those hammock nets for stuffed animals. The box said that it stretched to seven feet and I was later disappointed to learn that seven feet of netting doesn't come close to wrangling in our stuffed zoo. William could comfort an entire hospital ward with all the little shit he has.

He is such a collector. His top dresser drawer contained just about everything but clothes: Christmas bows, birthday cards, a lone checker, a few orange Tic Tacs, pennies, bottle caps, the tie he wore to Grandma Jean's funeral, three wallets, fuzzy key chains all scattered about. I might need to nip his love of rummage sales in the bud.

I spent at least ninety minutes trying to fix the dresser drawer. I tried everything I could think of, even praying to the Ikea Gods. Finally, fed up and tired, I punched the drawer. It slid open and I discovered the loose screw that started it all. I thought it was ironic that it opened with force and anger; all the gentle pleading I had done, ignored.

So now, neatly folded clothes have replaced William's treasure box (really, a visit to his dresser is like getting to pick a toy out at the dentist). Near the end of the day, just as I was sweeping the last of the dust bunnies (no more rotten fruit) into the trash, I heard a crash outside and Lizzie came running. She screamed, "Someone is lying dead on the street," but what I heard over the roar of the window air conditioner, was "Daddy is dead in the street." I teleported to our front yard, heart in throat.

It was not Daddy. It was a young woman, hit at full speed by a silver car. Her cotton candy-pink bike was cut in two pieces; she had hit the windshield of the car and was not moving. Ambulances, police, and a flashing yellow fire truck lined the street. She did not die.

I had been very crabby cleaning the kids' room, which even clean doesn't look clean. The accident put the room into perspective and seemed to be yet another reminder to me this week that change can be as sudden as it is slow. If there are angels up "there" trying to get me to understand this, point made. I get it.

August 20

When I first started teaching, I loved the drive to school. As I hadn't had children yet, I wasn't used to being up early, so even when school started at the end of August, it felt like autumn: the morning air was cold and promising. The whole world smelled like school. Once Luke was born and early mornings became mandatory, the drive to school lost its magic.

We start up again next week and more than ever before, I am dreading it. How many times can a human being experience the first day of school and still feel joyful? Where the rhythm of the school day, marked by bells and green hall passes used to provide a steady beat for me, it now feels like white noise.

Even if it is only an occasional flutter, I think that the nervous-butterflies-in-stomach feeling is a sign that you are enjoying your work and that you are doing what you are born to do. Tonight, Luke got a call from the Milwaukee Repertory Theater that they would like him to audition for *A Christmas Carol*. After an initial "YES" response, excitement overflowing, the butterflies visited him big time. I had a painting teacher once who asked me how I knew whether or not my painting was finished and I told him that it was finished when I could say "Ta-Da!" He agreed and said, in his slight Italian accent, "Yes, yes, it's when your stomach is smiling that you know."

I am wondering if all the signs I've been receiving about change lately are preparing me for something grand. Even the fortune wrapped inside my cookie last night read, "Something wonderful is going to happen to you soon." I'm not kidding. I am hopeful that this is the case and that the signs are not preparing me for some sort of devastation, some sort of, "See? I warned you to pay more attention," kind of thing.

I think, however, that I have stopped believing in a blueprint. I've started to believe, to understand deeply, that every single millisecond is about my own choosing. In a few ways, that has thrown me into a bit of a funk; it's a deer in headlights kind of feeling. Replacing the belief that "something wonderful will happen to you soon," with "Create something wonderful now," is, unfortunately, slightly more complicated than I'd like it to be.

The word "leap," comes to mind. I love that word. Launching with joy and hope, with nothing to pack but oneself. If I think about my narratives turning into sitcoms, I get butterflies. If I think about my illustrations bound in a magazine tossed on a coffee table, I get butterflies. If I think about my picture and name heading up a column, I get butterflies. My stomach doesn't just smile. It grins.

August 22

When I picked up Elizabeth from her friend's house this morning, she was leaning over an orange inner tube filled with found toads. The girls were very excited, as they had "rescued" the tiny things from the pool and made a home for them in the plastic tube, which was now filled with Barbie toys, cattails, leaves, and some water. They named the fat one "Chubino," a play on her friend's last name. Elizabeth was taking one of the toads for a walk in a stroller that was smaller than my palm.

I love watching Elizabeth with her girlfriends. They scoot about the yard in their matching ponytails and bikini's, their entire beings screaming summer and friendship. William was with me when we arrived at the house and he watched the toad festivities from a distance, quietly. Lizzie is his confidant, his older sister, his friend, and she is making connections that he can't quite reach yet.

I could not write yesterday, but not because there wasn't a lot to say. I had an early morning session with Martina and it wiped me out, both emotionally and physically. It's difficult to write about the experience without sounding corny, but the energy healing session quickly progressed into a past life regression/soul clearing and I ended up sobbing so many tears that I felt exhausted and distant, enthused and depressed simultaneously. I guess the details aren't so important, except to know that my connection with William runs very deep, so deep that it haunts me.

As I observe him, standing shyly in the corner of the yard, watching his sister play with abandon, listening to her giggle as she joins arms with her girlfriend, my heart just swallows him up.

Tonight, when I tucked him in bed, I told him a story about four girls, six toads, and a shy boy. The toad spied the boy from the corner of his eye and, near the end of the tale, hops to the dimple on the boys cheek and kisses him, leaving behind a giant blue jelly bean that tasted like blueberry pie. William loved this story, as he does all the ones I make up, the more absurd, the better. He is my storyteller, to be sure. He watches the world more intently and with more accuracy than most ninety year olds have cumulatively.

Details matter to him. A year from now he will probably ask me to tell him the story about the toad and the pie and I won't recall what he is talking about. What I like about this is that I have always seen so much of Sean in him, but I am beginning to see me, the parts of me that I treasure the most - the private, vulnerable self, the one that remembers and retraces. The more I know William, the more I know myself. For that, I am pretty grateful.

August 23

Recently, Mary told me that eight hours of sleep was not important, but that my belief system was making sleep essential. If I stopped believing that sleep was essential, I would no longer really need it. In other words, sleep is overrated. I'm not quite sure about that, but I do know that I am happier at two in the morning than I am at other parts of the day. If I didn't need to teach or get my kids up for school, I'd be more than content to rise around eleven and stay up until the wee hours of the morning. Societal norms are really fucking up my flow. The best part about summer is that I never have any idea what day it is. In four days that will all change and I'll start going to bed at ten again, before *The Daily Show* even airs. I'm going to need to get TiVo.

Even though summer is coming to a rapid halt, I am eager for cooler weather, jeans, sweaters, boots. Enough of this short sleeve crap, however, I do have to say it's nice when the kids don't have to spend forty minutes finding hats, mittens, scarves, backpacks. I told a friend that I wasn't looking forward to the morning routine again. She replied that the one thing she was dreading was making lunches, to which I groaned in sympathy.

The worst part is that the kids aren't allowed to bring sugar or salt at their school, so packing lunch gets to be quite the challenge. No chips, lots of fruit. What pisses me off about that whole thing is that if the kids get hot lunch, they get things like hotdogs. Elizabeth got reamed out for bringing Vitamin Water once, but the kid next to her was eating pizza. If my kids would agree to eat the hot lunch, I'd kiss the cafeteria floor. Once, though, the school served stroganoff and that did them in for the rest of elementary school. Try eating salt-free stroganoff and you'll empathize rather quickly. Even their teacher passed around some granola bars after lunch, as a gesture of compassion.

It's been a full day. Luke tried out for the play at the Rep, I signed Lizzie up for a hip-hop dance class, and debated between karate or gymnastics for William. The kids went swimming with Sean, and later Sean and I went out to dinner with about fifteen other parents from the kids' school. I came home and made a purse and did laundry, and now am here, gazing at this screen, completely unconcerned and unaware of what time it is, though I do believe it's almost three.

It has been busy, yes, yet I have been feeling very distant and introverted. Even engaged in conversation, laughing over drinks, sewing a flawless seam, I know that I am somewhere else entirely. I don't know how to reel myself back in. Am I protecting myself or just bored?

Yesterday, I opened my car door to a lovely waft of onions and pickles. William had his first Wendy's cheeseburger and did not like the condiments. Instead of putting them back in the white bag, he shoved the onions in the door handles and put numerous pickles under each seat. After a night in eighty-degree weather, they were definitely ripe and even those of us who like pickles will not be eating them for quite some time. I bought new floor mats, an air freshener, car cleaning spray, etc. I scrubbed the car for hours until it looked like a shiny hand-me-down. Earlier in the day, I had a migraine headache that had started around 5 a.m. The most relaxed I have been for weeks was sitting in my car, scrubbing away a summer of beach sand and yellow mustard. Maybe Mary is right. Maybe it's not the sleep that is important, as long as there is a time in the day that feels like I own it. Here's hoping that I can own something more exciting than events that directly involve Lysol and paper towels.

August 24

Today was the last Sunday volleyball party of summer. Every Sunday, we head over to the house of a friend of Elizabeth's, with several other families, to watch the kids swim and jump on the trampoline, as the adults play volleyball and drink wine. We usually leave mosquito bitten, tired, and happy.

Sean played volleyball yesterday, while I stayed on the deck and chatted to the other two mom's on "pool duty." Each time Sean dove for the ball, everyone on the opposing team would yell "KITCHEN," to throw him off and simultaneously to tease him about our incomplete kitchen project. At one point, I walked over and sat on a blanket to watch the game and a ball came flying at me. I ducked. Two of the men joked that had I hit it, they would have come over to finish the kitchen for Sean.

It did not dawn on me until we drove away that this is the first group of friends that Sean and I have made together. Usually it's just my friends or his friends and the other person tags along. Though I'm still not sure I'd be invited to any of these events if it weren't for Sean, whose charisma and charm are a bit more inviting than mine might be. For years, when the kids first started school, we'd joke about how every time a school parent met me after having first met Sean, she or he would say in a very surprised and disappointed voice, "Oh. *You're* Sean's wife?" Then the person would inspect me for a while to see if there was something special that they just couldn't see initially.

The whole thing reminded me of the *Curb Your Enthusiasm* episode where Cheryl leaves Larry and all of their friends, even their favorite restaurant host, begin to exclude Larry David from everything because they "chose Cheryl." My favorite line from that whole episode is when Larry asks Ted Danson why he wasn't invited to his oceans fundraiser. Ted Danson looks over Larry's head and says, "Oh, well, I thought you were our global warming guy." I love that.

I have a feeling that in this new circle, Sean is the oceans guy.

August 25

Today would have been Grandma Jean's birthday. Lizzie asked if we would be having a party if Grandma were still alive and I told her no, that my grandma was not much one for parties or crowds. My favorite photograph of her, however, is one in which she is newly pregnant and at a Christmas party. She wore a tiny sleeveless satin dress, dark, shiny, hair in a bouffant up-do, a cigarette in one hand and a cocktail in the other. She looked like Jackie Kennedy in that shot, but happier.

She died only sixteen months ago and there have been so many times that I would have liked to have called her to tell her about something, like yesterday when Elizabeth said that she wouldn't buy candy at the store because she was trying to be healthy and then added, "So I'll just have soda." I would have liked to show her the pictures of William learning to ride his bike or the video of Luke performing the pharaoh. I know she would have watched that video a thousand times.

There are things that remind me of her: lemons, coffee yogurt, Hagaan Daaz ice cream (boysenberry and coffee mixed up), Sara Lee banana cake, schaum torte, cozy ankle socks, soft blankets, TV guide, Hugh Jackman. For her last birthday, I brought her soap and lotion, and tea, in a little brown bag from the organic co-op. William and I visited her. I didn't realize that it would be her last birthday, though if I had, what would I have done differently?

We couldn't visit her today, not possible. Instead, we spent the day with Lolo. We had pedicures and lunch and she bought the kids some stuff at Old Navy. We walked the length of the

147

mall, which took just about forty minutes, at her pace. She told everyone, from the woman doing her nails to our waitress, that she is ninety-one and was satisfied that the waitress commented that she was doing "damn good" for that.

She held on to my arm as we walked, her hand shaking the whole time. I wondered if she ever feels depressed about how much she has slowed down. Are there days that she just wants to be done? At what age do people start thinking about their "lasts": last pedicure, last haircut, last movie, last Christmas? For Grandma Jean, it was different because she prayed for lasts. She was in so much pain most of the time, that I believe she would have said, "Please GOD, LET THIS BE MY LAST CHRISTMAS!" Even though we miss her, her death came as a heavy sigh of relief to those of us who loved her most. For Lolo, it will be different.

It's already starting to get dark by eight o'clock, the nights just a teeny bit colder than usual. Tomorrow is my last day of summer vacation. As Lolo and I head into fall, her toenails dark pink, mine so purple, they look black, I wonder how many lazy summer Monday afternoons we will have left, or if this, perhaps, was our last one.

August 27

I woke up a few nights ago with intense lower back pain. I remember having some low, dull pain a week or so ago, but this was different. The sharp pain woke me up in the middle of the night and continues to get worse, which most likely means that I have another ruptured ovarian cyst. It's no coincidence that this event has coincided with the first day back at school.

What would Martina say? I imagine that she would tell me to breathe and to ask my body what it is trying to tell me. Martina doesn't believe in coincidence either.

When I breathe, at first, I hear all sorts of complaints about how the first day back went. There were fifteen construction workers in my room, drilling a big hole for an elevator. Dust was everywhere, the noise was excruciating after a bit. I could not hear my colleagues. I had to unpack four towering skids of art supplies. I tried, really tried, to wrap my head around teaching the new digital imagery course, but my head just didn't open that much. At lunch, I felt disengaged and removed from the typical first day banter. After lunch, I picked up my new ID badge, only to see that I was orange and that my face filled most of the frame. I also noticed that there is now a gap in my teeth where there didn't used to be. I have been teaching in the same building for twelve years and my name was misspelled on my computer login. My phone extension changed without anyone telling me and I cannot retrieve my messages. I forgot my code for the copy machine. Like Judith Viorst's children's book hero, Alexander, it was a terrible, horrible, no good, very bad day, which concluded with going to a technology meeting at the kids' school that communicated new policies to which I oppose, but was too tired to question.

Still, it was just one day, and as I breathe deeper, I know that my back pain doesn't have much to do with it. It's bigger than that. Starting the school with the house in shambles is part of it. Not being able to conclude the day around a home cooked meal is part of it. I have outgrown my fishbowl.

August 28

Tonight Barack Obama accepted the democratic nomination for president in front of eighty-five thousand people and millions of T.V. viewers, including my three children, who watched it with me on the couch. The boys were bookends, William nestled into Greta, Lizzie nestled into me in the middle. When Obama walked onto stage, I cried and William, ever the little Montessorian, ran upstairs to get his deck of president playing cards.

Right before the big speech, we had been discussing who our current president is. Will had to rummage through the portraits of past presidents to see what Dick Cheney looked like as I futilely explained that Cheney was a vice president, not a president, and even if he were a president he wouldn't find him in that deck, as the last one in the set ends with Clinton. Still, William couldn't help but giggle at the name "Dick," and Lizzie wanted to know if Dick Cheney (the recent Olympics still fresh in her mind) was Chinese.

They settled down eventually and we watched the forty-two minute speech. It dawned on me that the only president since my youngest children have been born has been Bush. I was home with William on a maternity leave on 9-11. I remember rushing back from walking Luke to school, where another mom had told me about the two planes, worrying about my brother as I raced the double stroller for six blocks. I was glued to the T.V. for weeks: the celebrity sing-a-longs, the day time talk shows, David Letterman's return to Late Night. One of the women whose husband called her from his cell phone on the plane was named Lizzie.

151

Again and again, I watched the planes crash into the towers. As I held my newborn in my arms, pacing back and forth in front of surreal images, I remember wondering what kind of world I had brought him into. I even remember flashing back to *All in the Family* episodes in which Meathead Michael argued with Archie about how procreating in a world that is overpopulated is irresponsible.

Watching the speech tonight made me feel like I had brought my children into a world rich with wonder and possibility, and it was the first time in eight years (and maybe in my lifetime) that I have felt truly proud of my country. I understand why people fight for it now, in a way that even yesterday, I took for granted.

The boys fell asleep by the end of the acceptance speech. When I clicked off the television, I asked Lizzie what she thought Obama was saying in that speech. "No idea, really," was her response. I wonder if she'll even remember sitting here with me, or my insistence that she watch such a historical moment, or that I took her out of school one day last spring to attend a rally. Will she grow up under Obama's lead and will that make all of the difference?

August 29

August 29th: Vaginal Probe Day. So I finally gave in and called my ob-gyn about the ridiculous back pain. I have been putting it off, but it finally got too bad to ignore. His nurse said to come in around ten, which would be before his first appointment. I wondered what it would be like to start my day, everyday, by doing a vaginal exam on a stranger. I took the appointment because the thought of going to the emergency room was worse. That's what happened the last time I had this and the ultrasound technician might as well have been playing field hockey in my vagina. I think she had forgotten that her "wand" was not a Nintendo joystick, moving my ovaries around, eager to advance to the next level of her game.

I figured I could avoid the probe altogether, by just having the exam in the doctor's office, but no, after the exam, he wrote a prescription for the ultrasound. I called the outpatient office as soon as I got home, which ended up to be a very awkward conversation because our living room windows are open and it is Harley Davidson's one hundred-fifth anniversary, so motorcycles va-va-ROOM down our busy street all day, constantly, until even my cheeks vibrate. Anyway, it was so loud that I had to keep repeating myself to the appointment scheduler lady:

"What is the appointment for?"

"An ultrasound."

"For what?"

"For pain."

"What does the slip say?"

"Vaginal probe."

"What?"

"Vaginal probe."

"What?"

"VA-GIN-AL PROBE."

"What symptoms are you having?"

I had to stop myself from screaming, "Aren't you just the appointment scheduler? Why do you need to know this?" However, with the screeching motorcycle noises, I figured I just better get through the call, so I said, "Ovarian cysts."

"What?"

"Ovarian cysts!" I don't know why I didn't shut the windows at this point. We were finally able to make an afternoon appointment, which I showed up for late (went to the wrong office first) with a full bladder, as instructed.

This time, the ultrasound technician was very nice, a lovely June Cleaver type who complemented me on my ability to hold a lot of pee. "Oh my, you do have a full bladder, good girl," she said as she pushed her "mouse" around some warm KY jelly that she had spread, like mayonnaise over my stomach. After about ten minutes, she instructed me to go pee and to undress, "Robe open in the back. You can bring your clothes out here because there is no hook in the bathroom." She waited outside the door and listened to my five-minute release. When I came out she was smiling at me as if I was her daughter coming home from my first day of school, "Feel better?" she asked.

I scooted onto the table and she started her wand work. She wasn't crazy like the first girl, who moved that wand like a child furiously scribbling crayons on paper. This woman moved pretty slowly and precisely. We talked about the weather and the size of my ovaries at the same time: "It's so gorgeous out. Oh look! One of your ovaries sits right on top of your bladder," and so on. I can't imagine how weird that must be, probing strangers hour after hour, week after week. I can't imagine jumping out of bed in the morning to go to work: "Oh, boy! More vaginas!" This lady seemed to like her work though. She was a fine mix of calm meets perky and didn't seem at all curious or concerned to be staring at my insides to which she stared at, instead, as if my uterus was a fish bowl.

Ultimately, the test confirmed that yes, there is a lot of fluid in my uterus, pressing on my spine, so I filled my prescription for Perkaset and headed home, and sighed, knowing that I am probably more like the first, crazy ultrasound girl than I am the June Clever version.

August 30 and 31

We went to a party last night. It was fine and fun, though I didn't hold my promise to myself that if politics came up, I'd just be quiet. I prefer to hang out with people who can express an opinion or two, but I secretly admire people who can just remain neutral, calm and collected during philosophical disagreements, like Switzerland, but in human form. Maybe I should take a sabbatical next year and just hang out with the Swiss.

Speaking of the Swiss, this summer I have developed a taste for swiss cheese. I have never cared for it much, but now I eat it all the time. I keep making bagels with spicy mustard, pickles, and baby swiss cheese.

Susie and I went to Sam's Club today. It was my first visit there and for a while, I had twenty dollars worth of swiss cheese slices in our cart, until I thought better of it and traded it in for grapefruit cups. Susie bought a jar of pickles that was as tall as the average two year old; it was only four dollars! It was so bizarre to walk around that place. It's the Ikea of bulk grocery shopping, except that they also sell tires and televisions, Calvin Klein jeans, and school supplies.

Susie is single and has lived by herself for twenty years. I don't know if she has ever shopped for five people before and as I loaded up our cart (which we pushed together, purses in the space where toddlers go) with sixty rolls of toilet paper and giant crates of animal crackers and juice boxes, I asked her if shopping with me was good birth control. We laughed and marveled at how one could purchase twenty giant rolls of Mentos for eight dollars. She cringed at the marachino cherries and I made a face at a giant can of brown pudding.

At Sam's Club, just like at Ikea, they don't have any bags for bagging, so we wheeled our oversized cart brimming with an enormous box of black forest ham to my "mom car". We unloaded my stuff, leaving Susie's pickles and her own set of grapefruit cups alone at the bottom. We parted ways. She called me minutes later, shouting, "You forgot your ham! You forgot your ham! Come back."

My hope is that this stuff will last and that I will be able to pack lunches for several consecutive weeks without interruption. I have a feeling that my kids are like goldfish. They'll eat whatever is in sight until it's gone, no matter how full. Instead of saving money and trips to the grocery store, I'll just end up with bloated, fat children. I did buy five hundred sandwich bags, so unless the kids start eating those too, we have no chance of running out anytime soon.

I am already regretting not getting that cheese.

September 1

Lunches are packed. New backpacks and shoes line the radiator by the front door. First day of school outfits are spread out on the bedroom floor and as Elizabeth and Will fall asleep, they argue about who will get to take a shower first.

William wanted beets in his lunchbox. Now there is a moment that I wish all the other moms could see: while other kids are taking processed cheese crackers out of their lunchboxes, my son will be happily eating away at his freshly steamed beets. "How *does* she do it?" they will ask. "My son won't even eat carrot sticks." I will not tell them that when William was three, I told him that beets were the candy of the vegetable world and that they would turn his pee red if he ate them. I'm sure he can't wait to show off his red stream to his first grade buddies: way to make a first impression.

At our in-service last week, our administration brought in an improvisational comedy group to warm up the teacher crowd. They told us that they loved performing for teachers, only second to nurses who tended to be a bit raunchier. At one point they asked the crowd to shout out lines of advice they would like to give their kids on the first day of school and a middle school teacher screamed out, "Wear deodorant!" I'll be sure to pass that along to Luke tomorrow morning.

Luke just told me that he needs me to iron his shirt for tomorrow. I told him that it's going to be ninety degrees tomorrow and he won't need long sleeves. "But, Mom," he insisted, "I want to look *good*." When he was eleven, the idea of looking good didn't cross his mind. Apparently, sixth grade has new standards. Unlike Luke, who didn't care what he looked like for over a decade, Lizzie has been preparing for her grand entrance all day. She asked me to paint her nails to match her shirt. That's what I get for taking her along for a pedicure when she was five.

I guess I'm ready too. I typed up first day assignments today for both Digital Imagery and for Illustration. Copies of supply lists and classroom procedures are photocopied and ready to go. My heart's not in it yet, but I am ready.

In college, an instructor told me that the way I was painting (abstractly, at the time) wasn't genuine. She said that it was like knitting for me: I knew how to make it look pretty, but I didn't believe it. That's kind of how I feel about teaching today. I'll do a hell of a job, I'll even feel engaged and inspired now and again, but most days, I'll just be knitting. Knitting well, but still . . . craft vs. art. I will remember what Mary said: "Distract yourself." I can do that. I can teach while I wait for the rest to come. I just want a sign that tells me when it's time to put the needles down; I don't want the scarf to be too long.

September 7

With school officially starting, I have realized that it's a bit trickier to write every day, especially since there was a scheduling glitch and I am teaching six classes a day instead of five. Even part time, that's eighteen classes in three days. I suppose that people who haven't taught before don't think that's a big deal. Sean says, "So what? You've been teaching forever, it's like putting on old boots."

When I first realized that I'd have the extra class, I felt overwhelmed. I didn't know how I'd teach from eight to two thirty straight: six different classes, one hundred and fifty kids, and no time to pee. So far, I've only had one full day of it and to my surprise, it was kind of fun, even though it was crazy. It felt a little bit like being on *The Amazing Race* or that episode of *I Love Lucy* where Lucy and Ethel are on the assembly line. When I was finished, my voice was hoarse and my eyes were glazed over, but my heart was racing and I felt exhilarated.

Time, in general, has been moving like racecars. I forgot how much I like getting back in synch with the rhythm of the school year. It's nice to have the kids in bed by nine. The house is quiet and we are all settled back in after a busy weekend.

Elizabeth and William started taking gymnastics on Saturday mornings. I've been there three times now and each time I get lost. This past Saturday, I drove around for an extra fifteen minutes, screaming my brains out, while the kids sat in the back with their eyes closed, hands folded at their lips in a prayer pose, mouthing "Please, please, please don't let us be late."

Last night, Sean and I went to a fortieth birthday party, which was held on a boat on Lake Michigan. We had a lot of fun. There was great music and lots of people. As I was getting ready to leave for the party, I asked Sean if I looked okay, and he said that I looked like somebody who sold candles on the street. I don't know what that meant, but figured that it was too late to change anyway and decided that I looked just fine. I must have because there was one girl at the party who was pretty fond of me and kept trying to sit on me. This made my other friend laugh really hard, so hard that she had to sit down to keep from peeing, because none of us wanted to use the "boat potty." We all danced, which wasn't like me at all, but I figured everyone was too drunk to remember what I looked like dancing, *and* as long as I already looked like a candle seller, I figured that hippie-patchouli scented-shawl wearing-hooped earring type girls looked nice dancing. Ultimately, we realized that someone's underwear was on the floor, but no one wanted to own up to whose they were, as they weren't nice underwear, but more like the kind you wear to the doctor's office.

We all hung out at the restaurant after the boat docked and four of us were craving Ethiopian food and were sad to realize that it was after ten and the Ethiopian restaurant was sure to be closed. Instead we settled for fries and salty things, drank water, and watched all the people from the party on the deck outside. I told one friend that something about the crowd made me feel old, but she said, "You're not old, you're just married."

I don't think that's it. I think it was more the realization that we were at a *fortieth* birthday party. Forty! And these weren't my parents' friends. Someone in my peer group turned forty. Sean liked being on the cruise so much that he said he wanted his birthday to be on a boat, but then I reminded him that his birthday is at the end of November and we live in Wisconsin.

161

Privately, I thought, "It seems like we just celebrated your thirtieth birthday," but then I remembered that William wasn't even born when we did that.

I don't really mind getting older. Forty doesn't haunt me or tease me with ideas of what I need to accomplish by then. The thing I struggle with is impatience, yearning for more, for all my wants to fall into place.

At the same time I want life to slow down long enough to notice it, or at least enough to find an hour in the day to record it. Until that happens, I might resign myself to writing once a week, or whenever the mood strikes, or perhaps, when there is a sense of urgency about it. Like I said, racecars. Part of me feels sad about that, or guilty maybe, as if I have been faithfully going to church for the past fifty-two weeks and now I've just decided to attend on holidays and funerals. So be it, for now.

I look back to the first entry of the summer and think fondly of the pigeon and I know that when I lifted my head up to the sky and screamed "Assistance, *PLEASE*," that it was given.

I am reminded of that old joke about the man who gets caught in a flood and scrambles up to the roof of his house:

> *Eventually a boat comes along and he is offered a ride to dry land, but he replies "Thanks, but I have faith that God will save me." The boat leaves to rescue others.*
>
> *The water rises higher and another boat comes along. Again the man rejects the offer of aid saying, "I*

have faith that God will save me," and that boat also leaves to rescue others.

The water rises to the point that the man is barely able to stay on the roof, clinging to his chimney. A helicopter flies overhead and lowers down a ladder, but the man again insists "I have faith that GOD will save me," and he does not climb the ladder.

Finally the man is swept away by the flood waters and drowns. When he gets to heaven he confronts GOD and asks "I had faith! Why didn't you save me?"

To which God replies "I don't know what more you wanted - I sent you two boats and a helicopter."

The tragic death of the pigeon released a flood of words in me at a time when I felt unsure about my ability to find my own voice. That day is a constant reminder to me that when I need help, I can ask for it out loud. Maybe next time I won't have to wait until I am flat on the ground, rain soaked and muddy, with a bird on my chest.

I knew when he landed on me that I had a story to tell. Since then, I have come to believe that if I pay close attention, I can receive offerings each day. I used to think that I would not ever really be an artist of much significance, as my life isn't full of sordid details or a painful past. This summer, each night since William offered a dying bird toast, I have sat in front of my computer to write. Sometimes this was easy because there have been obvious things to write about: a broken wrist, a vaginal probe, a pharaoh dressed like Elvis. Other nights, I would just whisper, alone in the dark, Word document waiting: "Something will come." A single pigeon convinced me that I create. I choose. I am.